EDUCATION IN THE 21ST CENTURY

EDUCATION IN THE 21ST CENTURY

Mohit Chakrabarti

Publications

KALPAZ PUBLICATIONS

Delhi-110052

Education in the 21st Century

ISBN: 81-7835-280-X

Published in 2007 in India by
Kalpaz Publications,
C-30, Satyawati Nagar, Delhi-110052
E-mail : Kalpaz@hotmail.com
Ph : 9811692060

Dedicated

To

V.N Rajasekharan Pillai,

Vice-Chairman,

University Grants Commission, India.

Contents

Preface

Education is a quest unending and exciting, fascinating and thrilling. It is a quest that promises growth and development in a systematic, harmonious and disciplined manner. It ensures excellence and ascent of humankind. Beset with countless problems and predicaments, education in the twenty-first century is poised with the non-essentials penetrating gravely into the heartland of humanity. Alarming are the finer sense and sensibilities of living in mutual response to goodness, sympathy and co-operation. Utter ukase, of course, there is in every sector of life—personal or social, national or global.

Torn between sectarianism, parochialism, poverty of higher vision of humane sensibilities and challenges of the appalling distress of humane enlightenment, higher education is deeply confronted with innumerable problems of humane askance and enquiry and, among these, affluence and utilitarianism, liberalisation and globalisation have brought forth unprecedented challenges from countless perspectives. "Challenges in Higher Education: Re-inventing right Avenues" is a consolidated and thought-provoking study towards this direction.

"Education and Challenges of Humanism" is a

penetrating analysis of some of the essential dimensions of humanism awaiting catholicity of vision in the cathedral of education. The components of humanism necessitate a fresh approach in the context of the needs and priorities of the twenty-first century. That education is an essential and perhaps unique vehicle of vibrant advancement of humanism has been critically elucidated.

Education, of late, has been undergoing unwarranted constraints in being bogged down as a commodity. Undeniably, the consequences are alarming for the uncompromising wishes and aspirations of a competition-crazy humanity. "Perils of Doling out Education as a Commodity" is an intensive study on some of the crucial parameters of education virtually pawned at the hands of abject consumerism and evasive attitude towards education for efflorescence of radical and revolutionary vision of life and the world.

Education sans accreditation of the right kind cannot but welcome futility. The education of the twenty-first century of which we can boast ought to be cradled and nurtured in total quality assurance in an ambience of an ideal and challenging learning and teaching climate well backed by quality administration, management, supervision and guidance programmes on study, research and dissemination. "Education and Accreditation: Exploring Avenues of Excellence" may be an illuminating contribution to understanding and appreciating the latest trends of assessment and accreditation in education.

"Re-Thinking Education for All" and "Motivation Education: Setting the Agenda for Quality Acceleration" may invite pregnant criticism from esteemed readers.

That evaluation of learners by means of examinations has already become a nagging nuisance is admitted by almost everyone concerned with education. "Reviewing Examinations" is an extensive analysis from different dimensions that may welcome further avenues of discussion at different levels of education.

Teaching teachers is nowadays one of the most delicate assignments where much has been expected and much denied and/or misused. Teacher education institutions, too, are wailing for minimum infrastructure facilities that may contribute to their efficiency and improvement in education. "Teacher Education at Crossroads" explores some of the vulnerable areas of teacher education, which may ignite more vibrant thoughts and possibilities of refinement.

"Tuning the School Climate" is a specific and suggestive study of education in relation to school climate. The education pupils receive in schools should be attuned to the favourable socio-aesthetic climate that is terribly lagging in many schools even in the twenty-first century. "Tuning the School Climate" is a concrete and suggestive analysis of some of the splendid and not yet trodden avenues of fine-tuning the school climate.

Education sensitised in values is education adorned in elegance. "Value Education for Socio-Aesthetic Excellence: The Indian Context" may be a pointer to the apposite role of education for cultivation of perennial values for effulgence in fullness.

I am abundantly indebted to Professor V. N. Rajasekharan Pillai, Vice-Chairman, University

Grants Commission, India, whose rich observations on education in the present century in general and education for assessment and accreditation in particular have greatly inspired me in writing this book. I humbly dedicate my work to him as a token of my profound reverence to him.

I would like to record my deep sense of indebtedness and appreciation to Sobdo Chakrabarti, my son, for his sincere assistance in computer work. I would also like to appreciate the continual support with warmth of thrilling enthusiasm received from Pranati Chakrabarti, my wife, all through my work.

If the book is cordially received by the respected readers everywhere and presents me with constructive criticism, I would muse the words of Rabindranath Tagore in delight:

I know not why today my life is all astir, and a feeling of tremulous joy is passing through my heart.

—*Gitanjali*

Seemantika **Mohit Chakrabarti**
Seemanto Palli
Santiniketan-731235

1

Challenges in Higher Education: Re-inventing Right Avenues

Higher education in India has already become confusing, elusive, aimless, job-shy and defeating. With continual erosion of values with regard to accessibility of the higher norms of intellectual efflorescence in every walk of life, it is alarmingly veering towards passivity, redundancy, desolation, disappointment and dullness. Today's higher education in India is plagued with innumerable predicaments: overemphasis on theoretical aspects of knowledge, absence of synchronisation between the theory and the practice of each and every knowledge item, lack of devotion to explore and examine newer strategies and experiences, carelessness in comparing and contrasting multidimensional avenues of ascent and excellence in advancement of learning and, above all, disinterestedness in judiciously negotiating the challenging realities of life.

Apart from the fact that higher education is yet to open up the diverse windows of knowledge explosion that makes room for interchange of ideas and ideals in a desirable and effective manner, the so-called advancement of learning pursued in our institutions of higher education more often than not fails to negotiate the immediate necessities of life, the essence and excellence of education notwithstanding. That quality in higher education is a myth nowadays and falls far short of the minimum expected standard of achievements is hardly denied. The crisis in higher education is the crisis of quality that guarantees our passports to inner vision and awareness to what we ought to be from where we are in order to be justified to our very being from mere becoming as is the hapless outcome now. Indeed, it is very unfortunate that higher education loses this quality consciousness and allows education that is rest assured with apparent adjustments with so-called professional competence. For reasons best known to the planners of higher education it is sheer toying with the aimless principles and perspectives of education in general and higher education in particular.

Deterioration of quality in higher education in our country is due primarily to four reasons. First, the exodus in higher education in the post-independence era has practically ignored or rather sacrificed quality and allowed a liberal and open entry to the *alma mater.* Consequentially, this rush in higher education has made education for research and innovation, creative and critical thinking a matter of secondary importance. Secondly, whatever quality is either sought or pursued in higher education very often runs dry because the incentives are few and far between.

Thirdly, lack of coordination between higher education and vocational education has scarcely allowed quality to have its natural and spontaneous efflorescence. Fourthly, a certain tendency of streamlined education has also affected quality in higher education so much so that it simply caters to the immediate priorities of bare living and loses sight of the deeper and more challenging involvements of life. That all policies and programmes of higher education necessitate a thorough overhauling in terms of qualitative teaching and learning should be the fundamental end-in-view of higher education anywhere and everywhere.

Leaving aside the fact that the much used (abused?) streamlined and fact-happy system of higher education is hardly a deviation from the filtration theory of education imparted in pre-independent India, what a mess is going on by mushrooming the bewildered youth of our country in almost forcing them to register their names in hapless colleges and universities where in the name of entry to the altar of higher education the most precious and vital years of life are more or less wasted in utter and appalling silence! To be happy and assured with the exercise and outcome of mere pen-paper-pencil test *sans* any innovations and experiments with real life situation may produce passive blockheads of mushroomed and mesmerised personalities but hardly responds to thrilling perspectives and promises of life. Who cares?

A radical and revolutionary approach to higher education should all the time encapsulate the visions and possibilities of making education the most apposite and living stream of the finer human sensibilities that profusely contribute to advancement of the global society. Institutions of higher education are, indeed, assigned with the ardent task of how to bring about a radical change in our concept of education not simply as a process of growth within but a vibrant means of leaning the invaluable lessons of love, sympathy and togetherness along with each and every component of humane and crystallised consciousness. When one thinks on sustainable development, one cannot but admit the fact that universities have a great role in synthesising and disseminating the best thoughts, best visions, best sentiments and best outcome of human erudition and experience in the most abiding and pulsating effulgence of perfection and brilliance. In the poignant words of the Delors Commission:

> As autonomous centres for research and creation of knowledge, universities can address some of the developmental issues facing society. They educate the intellectual and political leaders and company heads of tomorrow as well as many of the teachers. In their social role, universities can use their autonomy in the service of debate on the great ethical and scientific issues facing the society of the future, and serve as links with the rest of the education system by providing further learning opportunities for adults and acting as a centre for the study, enrichment and preservation of culture. There is increasing pressure on higher

> education to respond to social concerns, while the other precious and indispensable features of universities, their academic freedom and institutional autonomy, have also been the focus of attention.
>
> *Learning: The Treasure Within*, UNESCO Publishing, 1996, p. 131

How far have we responded to the functions of higher education as above?

Admittedly, quality conundrums in higher education are major contributors to utter ukase in the very march towards innovations best suited to the needs and priorities of academic advancement in general and fullness of personality in particular. We are yet to identify the basic reasons for deterioration of standards of achievements in dimensions of human endeavour. We are also far out of the target of accelerating the best intentions and possibilities of newer visions of knowledge and wisdom. We are yet to make a compressive account of the pitfalls of our very plans and programmes of activities well-calculated and backed by reliable, valid, suggestive, foolproof, scientific and critical backdrop of sustained endeavour so much so that higher education makes a distinctive paradigm-shift in our serene approach to education for ascent and excellence.

It may not be inappropriate to refer to the fact that the much desired paradigm-shift in higher education can assure miraculous progress in the attitude-shift of learners most of whom suffer from a typical learning complex that neither allows them to encounter the essential requirements of pursuing higher education nor leaves them to apply their saner visions and judicious decisions to be justified to their individual talents and identities. Again, those who enter the cathedral of higher learning become somewhat disillusioned and, more often than not, frustrated when they find that higher education is also restricted to the so-called success in or mere end-product of cramming, short-listing, manipulating, reviewing and, of late, muscle-flexing.

That the institutions of higher education are more or less subject to these dubious and shameful distinctions can hardly be exaggerated. It has been further and, of course, indirectly substantiated by the fact that the University Grants Commission has no way out but to introduce the National Eligibility Tests to ascertain and select eligible candidates who would be lecturers and/or junior research fellows. Surprisingly, nobody bothers about the huge national wastage of manpower and talents in repeating almost the same exercise in drilling with nearly the same syllabuses in almost all disciplines. This is not all. The over-riding spirit so glaringly reflected in the arena of higher education also enjoys political and national support in cleverly camouflaging the abracadabra of education and employment, which are yet to be earnestly synthesised.

Higher education can never ignore the burgeoning needs of pupil learning and pupil population. It must cater to the immediate needs and priorities of the society and at the same time be justified to the long term ends-in-view of education for a better and more enlightened humane society. When we speak of cultivation of higher knowledge and nobler sensibilities of life we cannot but involve ourselves in quest of a new culture where plurality of ethos and moorings may pave newer paths to the progress of human thoughts and human sentiments. The world has already come nearer to our doorsteps and our ignorance of this fact even now would definitely prize ourselves with narrowness of vision and decadence of inquisitiveness. We are, indeed, envious of a great heritage of higher learning well disseminated by world-renowned seats of higher education like universities of Nalanda and Taxila. That heritage rightly necessitates a revaluation in terms of apposite dissemination in course of extending the spirit of changing patterns of higher education.

Prior to making any significant approach to a thorough overhauling of higher education, what is right now needed is to bring about a radical and ruthless change in the pattern of teaching learning. Intensive use of information technology well accommodated to innovative strategies and thinking fillips in newer and wider domains of knowledge and experience would certainly pay worthy dividends to advancement of teaching as well as of learning. At the same time, apposite training of teachers and exchange of ideas and ideals from teachers of different disciplines in order to make higher education a thrilling, comprehensive and living experience of exercise of excellence is to be introduced with a positive and sustained approach. One might be aware of the suggestions put forward by the Report to UNESCO:

> At a time when the sheer quantity of knowledge and information is expanding exponentially and when higher education institutions are

confidently expected to be able to meet the learning needs of a constantly growing and increasingly varied student population, the quality of training for teachers and the quality of teaching in higher education institutions takes on ever greater importance. Higher education institutions have a key responsibility in training teachers, in establishing links with non-higher-education teacher-training institutions and in training teacher educators. They must open themselves up to bring in teachers from the economic and other social sectors to facilitate interchange between them and the education sector."

Ibid, p. 132

If higher education is the real determinant of a country's progress, a look back to older values well harmonised with the needs and priorities of the present era is not only desirable but also a pointer to our newer quest for rediscovery of man the unknown and the society yet to be a true representative of the global humanity. On the dawn of a new era of humane sensibilities and prospects of learning to live together in a conjoint and communicated aura of excellence and ascent of mankind, why not higher education be put and practiced in a new canvas of the aesthetics of erudition?

At the same time, higher education awaits a renewed vision and perspective from the regional to the global points of view. It cannot but take into account judicious overhauling of research activities and their social relevance side by side with the accreditation and cost effectiveness. In this connection, the recommendations of the Ramamurti Commission deserve special attention:

(i) In basic research it may not be really worthwhile to pursue and promote everything that seems interesting, important or feasible. The important criteria for the choice of areas should be promise of achievement of excellence and existence of special advantages that India or Indian scholars possess.

(ii) Where there is a potential for exploitation in the near or foreseeable future in the context of national needs and priorities, special effort should be made by supporting agencies, (in addition to encouraging basic research in relevant areas) to ensure possible exploitation of these results through establishing proper linkages with user (Economic Ministries or Industry) and undertaking programmes jointly with them.

(iii) In certain selected areas of research all efforts must be made to identify a few educational institutions where talented students and faculty could be attracted for pursuing well-planned advanced courses so that these institutions become the centres of excellence for teaching and research. Such centres should be well publicized and well-equipped so that the best of talent knows about the challenges and opportunities available to them. At these centres, critical-sized research groups should be established around outstanding scientists and engineers. Such centres of excellence should receive support from the Department of Education and the UGC as well as from other agencies for carrying out research. Resources available for such facilities should be adequate. Facilities of national laboratories located in the vicinity should be made fully available to workers in the universities, who together with the scientists of these institutions should take up joint post-graduate programmes and research wherever possible. (These centres are envisaged differently from the University Departments for which the UGC gives special support to turn them into Advanced Study Centres).

(iv) Science and technology agencies must support universities not only in the form of time-bound research projects but also in the setting up of sophisticated research facilities in educational institutions and providing such other infrastructural facilities which will attract the best of minds from all over the country. S&T agencies should provide certain proportion of overheads (say 20 per cent) to the institutions as part of the research grants. Without such overheads, the institutions will not be able to provide the infrastructure for high-quality research.

(v) It is important that research in humanities and social sciences is directed towards contemporary realities in the country. There is also need to initiate research which takes the Indian intellectual and cultural traditions seriously, not necessarily to accept them without question, but to learn from them in order to understand ourselves and to develop the composite culture of India envisaged in the Constitution.

(vi) We have to pay attention to those who aspire for careers in specialised areas of science, humanities, etc. since we do not have any undergraduate institutions imparting instruction of the highest quality, a few ones should be provided high-level support by the states and the UGC

> in order to enable talented and motivated students to get proper training and opportunities for learning.
>
> —*Towards an Enlightened and Humane Society*, Report of the Committee for Review of National Policy on Education 1986, Final Report, New Delhi, 1990, pp. 226-227.

Higher education should also emphasize on the fact that de-linking of degrees as an outcome of the socio-economic conditions of the country particularly in the context of spiralling unemployment problem has invited some crucial issues among which syllabus orientation, reshuffling of the contents and methodologies of teaching, infrastructure-analysis and evaluation, clarification of pupil intake capacity of educational institutions of higher learning, qualitative improvement of teaching and teaching personnel together with a desirable overhauling of the future prospects of such institutions from diverse directions deserve rethinking and judicious handling in right earnest.

Meanwhile, one of the major challenges of higher education is its appropriate democratisation. Unless effective steps are taken in negotiating some of the constraints of higher education among women, minorities and weaker sections, the whole process and possibilities of success of education as a means of national and global development turns out to be a flop. Some positive steps in this regard like understanding and sympathising with the right to higher education, extending facilities for higher study and research for scholars of the socially disadvantaged communities etc., would definitely work wonders in bringing about a fresh lease of life in making higher education truly dynamic and effective. As it is significantly suggested:

> The regional imbalance in the spread of higher education facilities affects the minority groups and weaker sections due to their perpetuating poverty levels as it disables them about going to other places for education. Hence there is a greater need to expand distance education facilities which can become easily accessible to them. In other words, preference must be given to these sections in enrolment in distance education programmes. The technologies, resources (books, journals, etc.) and the means for learning (study centres) through distance mode should be within their easy reach making them available in close proximity to either their place of residence or their place of work.
>
> There is a gap in the medium of instruction at the higher education level, particularly with reference to the weaker sections. This gap is more pronounced in case of students coming from rural areas.
>
> This gap is due to the fact that at the high school or PUC level, they do their studies though the medium of regional

languages while at the degree or post-graduate level they have to adjust to the English medium of instruction in many instances. In addition, there is a paucity of books in the regional languages at the postgraduate level. Also, often at the level of higher education, specially in the faculties of arts and social sciences, the lecture method becomes the first and last resort. To promote their enrolment and to sustain them at the higher education level, there is a need therefore:

(i) to re-orient the medium of instruction preferably to suit their earlier pursuits;

(ii) to produce good text books and reference books in regional languages; and

(iii) to supplement lectures with tutorials, seminars, remedial teaching sessions, etc.

Notwithstanding the controversy surrounding the minority rights given in the Constitution and their implementation, there is a need to interpret these rights to the advantage of the minorities, particularly by supporting them regarding admission at all levels, and enabling them to continue in these institutions until they complete the courses for which they are admitted. Such measures

> should actually benefit the minorities and nobody should be allowed to exploit the minority provisions for enhancing mercenary concerns. Only when these rights are interpreted and implemented in right earnest would the pious intentions with which they have been incorporated in the Constitution, be fulfilled. The barometer of their effectiveness is how each minority community person, who is denied education for reasons beyond his or her control, is helped in having an opportunity for education.
>
> —M. Khajapeer: "Democratisation of Higher Education in India with Special Reference to Weaker Sections, Minorities and Women", *Journal of Educational Planning and Administration,* National Institute of Educational Planning and Administration, New Delhi, Vol. X, No. 2, April 1996, pp.149-1

On the dawn of a new era of the twenty-first century, higher education is entrusted with newer challenges in diverse areas like education for women's empowerment, total eradication of illiteracy, quality assurance and excellence, national and global cohesion and so on. Together with these, the tougher challenges like apposite evaluation and accreditation in the light of Total Quality Management (TQM) need a renewed approach in the light of liberalisation and economic synergies. Meanwhile, the service of a new band of talented, innovative and diligent teachers in the universities and other allied altars of higher learning and research necessitates a total overhauling in the context of the present needs and priorities of an amazingly expanding and multidimensional global society. The challenges are, therefore, not only numerous and different but also complex and explosive. The major thrust areas may be tabled as follows

Table: I

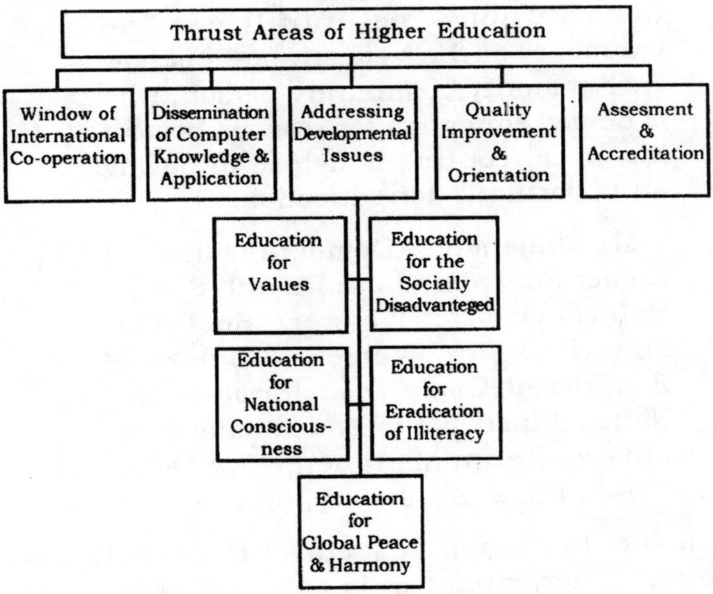

As a hallowed seat of higher learning, universities have a very important role in the study and dissemination of culture to foster newer meanings of human understanding and apprecia-tion. In this connection, the Report to UNESCO of the International commission on Education for the Twenty-first Century is significant:

> In addition to preparing large numbers of young people either for research or for specialised occupations, the

university must continue to be the fountainhead at which the growing numbers of people who find in their own sense of security a way of giving meaning to their lives may slake their thirst for knowledge. Culture should here be considered in its wider sense, ranging from the most mathematical of sciences to poetry, by way of all the fields of the mind and the imagination.

In this respect, universities have the specific features that make them especially favoured environments. They constitute the living repository of the human heritage, a heritage continually revitalised by the use made of it by teachers and researchers. Universities are usually multidisciplinary, making it possible for each individual to escape the confines of his or her initial cultural environment. They are usually more in touch with the international world than are other educational structures.

Each university should become an 'open' university, offering possibilities for distance learning and learning at various points in time. Experience in distance teaching has shown that, for people studying at the higher education level, a judicious mix of media, correspondence courses, computer communications technology and personal contact can broaden the options on offer at relatively low cost.

> These should include both vocational training and personal development courses. Furthermore, in keeping with the idea that each person should be both learner and teacher, greater use should be made of specialists other than faculty members: teamwork, co-operation with the surrounding community and community service by students are some of the factors that can enrich the cultural role of higher education institutions.

—*Learning: The Treasure Within,* UNESCO Publishing, 1996, p. 134.

Are we on the right track?

Education and Challenges of Humanism

- Is humanism at peril?
- Is man really the greatest annihilator of man?
- Is civilization an agony, an enigma, a dumb and doping state of human consciousness?

These and numerous other allied questions right now present humans with the unavoidable and unworthy ukase in sense and sensibilities enough to tarnish the image of man as the best of all living creatures. Lost is the vision of man who is altogether alone but not lonely in the world today where crisis of consciousness becomes a habitual and non-repellent part of one's being. Today's so-called humanism compromises with disastrous casualties more often than not careless of whatever qualifies and promotes man as the most apposite messenger of the All Serene.

Admittedly, man is now the lowliest and lost in man. The inner lotus land of man is being continually raped with rampant disgrace and dismay, reluctance and revenge, deterioration and destruction. Sweetness and light are replaced by rudeness and roughness. Meanwhile, in an arid land of virginity and impotence, the fertile seeds of humanism never find the favourable fountain of growth and freedom. Machines and automations are gradually becoming antagonistic and arrogant so much so that these are practically becoming less and less user-friendly to accelerate humane development—a typical breed of fundamentalism in science (anti-science?). Shaking slovenly and senseless hands with these is information technology, which has undeniably reached out its romantic and reckless wings with a vainglorious ecstasy: 'Mischief, thou art afoot'. The wailings of humanity are lost in the labyrinth of shameless mockeries of man and life.

Realiation of life in terms of soul-consciousness is even now a myth. In terms of humanism, education is now definitely at crossroads with the following askances:

- Whither exercise of the individual in quest of altruism which is the first and foremost lesson of humanism?
- Whither refinement of the self to march ahead for the beyonding of man which is the hallmark of humanism?

Apart from the fact that an individual as simply an individual alone is absolutely meaningless—*eka manushta sampurna nirarthak*— a truism so characteristically remarked by Rabindranath Tagore, the realization of the true identity of man the born humanist is gradually becoming elusive if not archaic. The more a person is involved in unmasking his/her personality—'extinction of personality' as T. S. Eliot would like to remind us—the more is he/ she nearer to the core of humanism *tyagenaikenamri-*

tatwa labhate, with renunciation and self-abnegation lies the prize of the nectar.

Simultaneously, the great lessons of humanism encompassing realization of truth, harbouring love and sympathy, nursling co-operation, care and simplicity, translating beauty in freedom of thought and action and similar other essential components of humane essence and excellence await re-vitalisation in our everyday ways and means of livelihood and allowing every human being to live *par excellence.* If one is not concerned with humanity in every affair of life and work, wherein else is the worth of oneself as a human being?

Undeniably, a serene catholicity of vision in solemn symphony with whatever is concerned with the march of humanism in all glory and grandeur ought to be everyone's earnest endeavour. Then, and then alone, the spirit of humanism finds the real aroma of efflorescence under all constraints and pitfalls notwithstanding. As Radhakrishnan adroitly elucidates:

> If we glance at the long history of India covering nearly five millenniums, we are struck by the contrasts of extreme situations, summits and chasms. The country rises, wavers, falls, shrinks into herself, tears herself to shreds and pieces and again endeavours to regain her greatness. She passes through different moods of pride, resignation, shame, detachment, excitement and adventure. Yet all through runs an idea which she is attempting to realize, a kind of equilibrium, a wholeness of human nature, which events and vicissitudes inseparable from all forms of life shake but do not shatter. The country is

> mobile in the surface but constant in the depths. India is a complex equilibrium with an extremely rich diversity. The country is not defined by any dominant race or religious doctrine or economic circumstances. We have a remarkable mixture of ethnical elements but the great tradition which has affected all her people is the work of human hands.
>
> — *The Spirit of Religion*, Pankaj Publications, New Delhi, 1980, pp. 116-117

What, then, are the practical approaches to tackling the diverse constraints that stand in the way of efflorescence and excellence of humanism?

- First, let there be an aggression of a different kind, which is long overdue. This is to totally eliminate hunger and poverty bereft of which humanism becomes a mere romantic weaving in the air.
- Second, eradication of deadly diseases and arresting pollutions of the environs of every kind everywhere awaits approaches and strategies afresh and anew.
- Third, replacing aggravating violence and hatred writ large in the global human society by love and non-violence is not only desirable but should be obligatory.
- Fourth, ensuring peace, justice and truth even under trying circumstances is the only alternative to negotiate ukase of every type, be it internal or external whatsoever or howsoever.
- Fifth, a certain pattern of stick-to-itiveness to whatever contributes to the advancement of aesthetic and humane sensibilities and nobler

visions of life in the grand welcome of truth, beauty and goodness of higher order is the dire need of the hour.

To translate the essential components related to the ends-in-view of advancement of humanism depends entirely on an individual's elevation to the apex of excellence beyond excellence. Therefore, the fountain of spiritual evolution as Sri Aurobindo looks forward to humanism of the right kind and of the right mind is the starting point of our quest for divine living. A dynamic re-creating of the individual from apposite perspectives of spiritual manhood is the yet-to-be-reached goal of humanism. In Sri Aurobindo's own words:

> For a spiritual society to come into being it is not enough that certain ideas favourable to the turn of human life should take possession of the general mind of the race. For the way that humanity deals with an ideal becomes almost an excuse for not living according to the ideal. More is needed: there must be a dynamic re-creating of individual manhood in the spiritual type. As will be the spirit and type of the individuals consisting it, so will be the realized spirit of the collectivity and its powers of life.
>
> —Sri Aurobindo: *The Human Cycle*, Sri Aurobindo Pathamandir, Calcutta, 1986, p. 83

The essence of humanism primarily depends on learning to live together. The education of worthwhile conjoint and communicated living is yet to find the real avenues for moulding and re-designing the destiny of mankind. Today's education must be one of alive and enlightened humanity in course of pursuit of knowledge that cares for making a fusion between the individual and the universal in terms of creativity and critical thinking. As Toynbee poignantly asserts:

> Every man, woman, and child that is alive today is living in a world in which mankind is now faced with the extreme choice between learning to live together as one family and committing genocide on a planetary scale. Neither the human race nor any living member of it can afford to ignore the present human situation. We must cope with it if we are not to destroy ourselves; in order to cope with it we must understand it; and trying to understand it commits each and all of us to making some acquaintance with at least three vast realms of knowledge: a knowledge of non-human nature; a knowledge of human nature; and a knowledge of the characters and histories of the local and temporary cultures—some relatively primitive, others relatively advanced—that man has created and transmitted and modified and discarded in the course of the ages that have passed since his pre-human ancestors became human. Formal education's minimum task has thus become a big undertaking in our day; and every child will have a strenuous course of formal as well as informal education to run in order to grow up into being an effective citizen of our new world.
>
> —Arnold Toynbee in Edward D. Myers: *Education in the Perspective*

of History, Longmans, Green & Co., London 1963, Concluding Chapter, pp.278-279

A certain pattern of humanizing education well suited to the needs and priorities of the global teaching-learning clientele is very well in agreement with disagreement in our recent operational strategies of education. And so, farewell to an ideal and very much desirable academic environment where shadow boxing has more often than not become the fundamental and forcefully prioritised intellectual exercise throughout an academic calendar. Between human and humane education, o, the difference!

Indeed, the challenges of humanism are the greatest symptoms and forewarnings of ceaselessly looking within and solemnly preparing for translating a new image of man:

> The awareness of values is the first step towards their actualisation. As the ancients knew, every man is born into the world fashioned by himself. What are we fashioning? To strive to leave behind a complete image of himself is the one vanity that man may be pardoned. Out of the clashing images on the modern scene, which shall we choose and why? Choosing is creating and in the revision of goals a new image is a priority.
>
> It will, first, be necessary to undermine a few myths. For instance, the idea that economic growth and conspicuous waste constitute progress; secondly, that it is man's duty and destiny to conquer nature rather than live in

harmony with the cosmos; thirdly, that Science and Efficiency (with a capital E) are the only way to fulfil the aims of civilisation.

* * * * * * *

Through the birth-pangs of a new world the tribal image of man is changing into the global, the universal man, *visva-manava.* Also towards an en ecological ethic in which hierarchy will not mean inequality and injustice. An open-ended, experimental image of both man and society, the Birthing of a Planetary Being, of possible selves and roles, is under way. It is indeed a long journey, not in the sense of a road already laid out, but, with every step, in the act of construction. Tread softly, for you tread on mankind's dream.

We *are* evolution. There must be nothing in the way of more-being and the coming civilisation, the ideal of human unity that should remain unattempted. Somewhere in a corner of our souls we all harbour the vision of a world in perfect integration, the paradise regained. Here is the undiscovered heartland of education which educationists have not much thought of. This is no doubt an act of faith, but it is a faith, which the highest Reason, the widest and the most patient reflection do not deny, but rather affirm. This creed is given, indeed, to humanity to support it on its journey, until it arrives at a stage of development when faith will be turned into Knowledge and perfect experience and Wisdom justified of her woks.

—Sisirkumar Ghose: "A New Image of Man", *Man and Society,* Intellectual Book Corner, New Delhi, 1977, pp. 98-103

Education for global interrelationship is the need of the hour. It is the only alternative to make a sensitised and harmonious relationship between man and man. It is the right road to awakening the true spirit of humanism among humans irrespective of caste, creed, colour etc. that have already done much mischief in the world of good sense and sensibilities, conjoint and communicated blessings of living together. As the Delors Commission appositely suggests:

> The first step towards grasping the growing complexity of world events and combating the feeling of uncertainty it endangers is to acquire a body of knowledge and then learn to put the facts in perspective and adopt a critical approach to the flow of information. Here, more than ever, education shows itself to be irreplaceable in developing judgment. It fosters a genuine understanding of events, going beyond the media's sometimes over-simplified and distorted portrayal. Ideally, it should help everyone to become, to some extent, a citizen of the turbulent and changing world that is being born before our eyes.
>
> There is obviously no way of understanding the world without understanding the relationship between human beings and their environment this does not call for a new subject to be added to the already

> crowded curricula but for existing subjects to be reorganised around a comprehensive view of the ties that bind men and women to their environment, involving both the natural and the social sciences. This type of training could be offered to everyone as part of life-long education.
>
> —*Learning: The Treasure Within, Report to UNESCO of the International Commission on Education for the Twenty-first Century, UNESCO 1996, p. 49.*

As knowledge is continually expanding and human life is fast becoming very complex and intriguing, education has now a bigger and much wider role to play. It opens a new horizon of understanding and appreciating individuals in terms of the universal goodness of mankind. At the same time, education plays a pivotal role in allowing and fostering an individual best nourished and enriched in a favourable climate of efflorescence. Thus the essence of individual ascent and excellence makes worthwhile contributions to the furtherance of humanism. As the Commission strongly suggests:

> Education must help to engender a new humanism one that contains an essential ethical component and sets considerable store by knowledge of, and aspect for, the cultures and spiritual value of different civilisations, as a much-needed counterweight to a globalisation that would otherwise be seen only in economic or technological terms. The sense of shared values and

> a common destiny is in fact the basis on which any scheme for international co-operation must be found.
>
> —*Ibid*, p. 50.

Education, therefore, cannot but create a new platform for advancement of human creativity. Human consciousness awaits a revision of values – a revision where designing with Nature is the first lesson to be learnt and cultivated in a war footing. Unless this is done education will fail to regain the lost paradise of eco-humanism. As it is characteristically remarked:

> The mature world-view will not tear man apart from Nature. Has not the Conquest of Nature turned out to be a defeat for Man? The distinction between *natura naturans* and *natura naturata,* cretive nature and created nature, has to be grasped once again. Art, one might say, does not merely reflect the visible; but, going back to the Archetype, reincarnates the invisible. The *milieu interieur* may be as important as any outward fact or event. Karma of the cosmos, pollution has proved at least one point; the erosion of the environment has followed the corruption of consciousness. As Wordsworth put it, the world is poisoned at the root. The moral is quite simple. Design with Nature must replace designs against nature. Today the milieu must be ecological, rather onto-ecological. Today's humanism is ecological humanism.
>
> Without a sense of the whole, responsible attitude towards man's total reality, "the universe is my

stupendous whole", we shall be lost. Man is both subject and object. What explains the crisis, the unease on the modern scene? There must be some grave error in our calculation. In the words of an Indian mystic, what we most suffer from in our outer life and its reactions upon our inner life is the imperfection of our relations with the world, our ignorance of others, our disharmony with the whole of things, our inability to equate our mind on the world with the world's demand on us. Without totality-thinking this is impossible. When and how our schizoid society will learn this simple lesson is anybody's guess.

Human creativity, if it is not to be an unwitting agent of a global farewell, must go back to the truth (dharma) of archetypal creativity. If this means laying aside the metaphysical barbarity of the past few centuries that is as it should be. The time has come to set the balance right, between the two sciences, of self and things. We shall be happier and freer without the incubus of a knowledge without wisdom. "I *am* a soul but I *have* a body", the paradox has never been fully solved. But this perhaps is the secret cosmic intention, the heart of the long journey. For every goal that draws us, the thing desired exists. In the energy of the earth is the soul of the universe. All energy is psychic energy, and the Energy an Eternal Delight—the discovery is sure to be made one day. The birth of the psyche is the key to an

> abundant life, of sacramental relationship, Edenic harmony, Adam's return to Paradise.
>
> —Sisirkumar Ghose "Creativity: The Ecological Challenge", *Meditations on Matricide,* Ajanta Books International, New Delhi, 1986, pp. 66-67.

To steer education towards enlightened humanism is always a challenge tough, complex, controversial, critical and counteractive. It needs an arduous and sustained preparation where the best inputs of human erudition and sensibilities await a very disciplined and serene approach. As already referred to, instead of alienation, the right road to advancement of humanism by means of education is cohesion between thought and action, contemplation and execution where the latest trends and techniques of science and technology are wedded to the world emotions and sensibilities best adorned with the invaluable ethos and moorings from time to time.

Education caressed in humanism is education for evolution of consciousness without which it loses its real identity. The soul of education is the education of the soul of humanism.

Do we believe, realise, re-think and act upon for the march of humanism by means introducing and participating in the endless task of vibrant education?

3

Perils of Doling out Education as a Commodity

Education is always an invariable incentive to self-awareness and self-esteem. When it becomes a commodity, matter-of-fact consumer goods as it is forced to happen in an over-ambitious profit-prone world of today, it very often loses the aura of excellence and the passion for pursuit of erudition and edification of mankind. Quite astonishingly, the recent trend in education pays more importance to steering it towards employment or whatsoever like this at the cost of quality, which ought not always to be assessed in terms of monetary or economic prosperity. The recent trend in education has also welcomed unhealthy competition that craves for material success and destroys the inherent essence of quest for wisdom.

Apart from the fact that we have already been warned against this disastrous tendency of 'buying' education by no less a celebrated document than the Report of the Kothari Commission way back in 1964 – 66 in the very opening chapter, we still haunt for making education a matter of money-grabbing avenue to part with real pupil- progress in terms of quality and excellence in education.

A recent survey of institutional earnings and expenditures in altars of education especially at the university level would certainly direct one to come to this conclusion that education for real and thrilling advancement of learning has been alarmingly left unnoticed .The recent decision to hike fees for students studying in educational institutions may puff up the avenues of earning but may not accelerate the avenues of learning since earning and learning are not necessarily mutually exclusive. In fact, who will care for the poor but meritorious learners or what will happen to those talented learners who will not be allowed to have their entry in educational institutions simply because of their appalling poverty?

Admittedly, education should be looked upon as an inseparable part of national pride, and in order to restore and thrive this national end-in-view, it should always be a matter of general concern for promotion of quality in education even with provision of desirable and satisfactory financial support. It may so happen that sometimes education may not be of money's worth. Even then, some sort of risk must be undertaken provided, of course, that there is a possibility of progress in education.

As our country's pupil-clientele vary from state to state, region to region and community to community in addition to the fact that there is a great deal of socio-economic differences, burdening pupils with hike in fees will simply deny quality education for a great chunk of learners and allow, on the other hand, a few affluent pupils to pursue higher studies and be well established in the society. This is simply negativism in education – a parochial approach that eliminates good sense and sensibilities so important for attainment and exercise of ideal citizenship. Moreover, this will rampantly aggravate communal tension and national disintegration.

Prior to launching any programme for hiking fees in educational institutions, the following deserve immediate attention:

(a) Adequate and proficient teachers are available throughout the session.

(b) The academic ambience is well supported by good library and laboratory facilities, regular and disciplined instructional climate, apposite programmes for pupil-evaluation, publication of results in due time, pupil-placement schedules for judicious occupational fulfillment, incorporating accreditation programmes and an integrated approach to multi-disciplinary and conjoint curriculum reconstruction.

(c) A scientific and foolproof survey of the felt needs and priorities for hiking fees.

(d) Setting up intensive study circles where celebrated thinkers, scholars and educationists congregate, deliberate and discuss on various issues concerning education for fullness.

(e) Publication of research journals containing recent trends and motivations in education for humane growth and development.

(f) Inviting individual learners and teachers to accelerate community and societal needs and priorities with a view to fostering national cohesion and solidarity, discipline and integrity.

(g) Empowering the new generation of learners and teachers to shape the destiny of man anew in keeping with the astounding advancement of global understanding and cooperation, peace, amity and excellence of humankind in diverse directions.

Admittedly, any hurried and sentimental approach to hiking fees for academic improvement by ignoring diverse burning issues in education would simply invite student unrest and unhealthy academic and administrative climate. It is high time to arrest such disorder to take place and cautiously break the camel's back in the altar of learning.

Meanwhile, a careful and cautious probe into the social and economic adjustments of parents with particular reference to the immediate social and economic environs may unfold better avenues of eliminating some of the crucial problems that very well stand in the way of humane and sensitized education for one and all. The problems with learners grilled in and served with sub-standard education have their roots in parents specially eking out livelihood below poverty-line, wherefrom the seeds of frustration and ultimately of discord and disintegration thrive in all plenty and embarrassment, thanks a lot to the utopian planning and execution of low-cost living under low income group formula.

Our educational institutions make sentimental and unscientific journeys to nowhere by claiming high fees in place of acceleration of the essential ends-in-view of looking after regular attendance, welcoming challenging academic demands and last but not the least peeping through the windows of hapless parents and guardians gasping under terrible inflation and economic crisis. At the same time, an economically viable plan and programme of education suited as best as possible to the needs and priorities of the learning clientele any time anywhere is the only alternative for fulfillment of the vision of education embracing the global community.

Meanwhile, education for the twenty-first century should cater to the individualistic age in such a way as to ensure an easy access from the individual to the universal ascent of humans. A developing humanity in the light of education as it is expected in the very beginning of the new century now is looking forward to fascinating dimensions in radical and revolutionary reassessment of ideas and thoughts, problems and possibilities. As Sri Aurobindo reminds us:

> The individualistic age, proceeding by individual mind and reason, however, must go from the individual to the universal. In Europe in modern times that has taken the form of physical science. But after a time it must become apparent that this is not the whole knowledge, that man is a mental as well as a physical and vital being. Therefore, to find the truth of things and the law of his relation to that truth he must go deeper and fathom the subjective secret of himself and things. This he may attempt to do for a time by the power of critical and analytical reason, but not for long. For in his study of himself he cannot but come face to face with the soul in himself and the soul in the world and find it to be an entity so profound, so complex

> and so full of hidden secrets and powers that his intellectual reason betrays itself as an insufficient light and fumbling seeker.
>
> All these tendencies are manifest in the world today. The art, music and literature of the world have also undergone a profound revolution in the direction of an ever-increasing subjectivism, from the vital to a mental, intuitional and psychic, pointing the direction in which the human mind is being piloted on a momentous voyage of discovery. This can be seen also in the new ideas about education and upbringing of the child.
>
> The nascent subjectivism shows itself not so much in the relation of individuals or in the dominant ideas and tendencies of social development but in the collective self-consciousness of man in the nation. It is here that we shall see most clearly what is its actual drift and the goal towards which the social cycle, entering this phase, is intended to arrive in its wide revolution.
>
> —Sri Aurobindo: "The Coming of the Subjective Age", *The Human Cycle,* Sri Aurobindo Pathamandir, Calcutta, 1972, pp. 9-11.

The role of teachers in arresting the perils of education as a commodity is undeniable. The lessons to be imparted ought to have a realistic and dynamic approach to eliminating socio-cultural and socio-aesthetic constraints well groomed in the nursery of economic ukase. Considering the fact that teachers are also the inseparable partners of the nation's progress, why not launch a socio-economically viable programme of orientation of teachers and teacher educators for exercising and implementing newer strategies of education for ensuring better and more humane enlightenment?

4

Education and Accreditation: Exploring Avenues of Excellence

Education is a means of fullness. It is a pointer to one's worth intrinsic as well as extrinsic of oneself in relation to others and vice versa. If one fails to educate for the cause of others, one ceases to be a human being. At the same time, if others in and around one do not care for the education of one who is an inseparable part of them as a member of one great family of man, whatever education is introduced becomes futile and meaningless. Hence, there is an immense necessity of appropriate and relevant assessment and accreditation in education.

Accreditation in education from a general overview of success and/or failure triggers absence of credibility and more often than not welcomes resentment and revolt. Such a general overview fights shy of the following:

(a) It is not psychologically negotiated.

(b) There is proneness of its being biased,

baseless, bolstered by vested interests and parochial.

(c) It affects pupil progress from different praxes.

(d) The motivational aspects in education are severely damaged.

(e) The finer components of education are left apart either ignored or unattended for exercise in proper ways at appropriate times.

(f) Pupil-interest in specific and different areas of knowledge, understanding, skill and appreciation suffers from evasiveness or indifference.

(g) Pupil-appreciation that invariably stands for positive avenues of self-analysis and manifestation hardly enjoys warmth of enthusiasm and approval.

(h) No proper and sufficient stimulation for advancement in education is available.

(i) Promotion for innovation or creative and critical thing is terribly jeopardised.

(j) No accountability of any sort is either registered or translated into sincere action.

(k) The aims and objectives of education are not justified in either contemplation or action.

(l) Pupil self-accreditation is discouraged or ignored.

(m) Teachers, with all sincerity of purpose and devotion to teaching notwithstanding, fail to address the grievances and wailings of learners.

(n) Institutional sanctity in teaching and learning is grilled by erroneous and faulty mechanism of assessment and accredita-tion, if any at all.

With nursing of education on the one hand and lopsidedness in carrying out minimum programmes of education on the other, accreditation has become of prime importance nowadays for improvement and acceleration in education. The recognition of an educational institution by making a scientific and foolproof assessment of its plus as well as minus points of instructional and other functional activities makes the concept of accreditation meaningful and transparent at the initial and fundamental stage. But all endeavour at accreditation is to fulfil the great mission in education that stands for advancement of learning and all-pervasive and all-embracing efflorescence of humankind.

For self-accreditation by an educational institution, two major strategies may be undertaken:

(i) Self-study

(ii) Self-evaluation.

The parameters of both self-study and self-evaluation are to be pre-determined in a preferably planned and phased manner with sufficient back-up components like environment opportunities and positive support together with manifold limitations as pointers of forewarning. Classroom climate and aesthetic fitness in addition to or absence of adequate hygienic conditions and economy of multipurpose use also serve as guidance to framing qualitative as well as quantitative network of institutional accreditation. Besides there are other areas contributing a lot to successful accreditation. The following Tables (Table A & Table B) show the different schedules under study for institutional accreditation:

Procedures of Accreditation : Institutional

Table: A

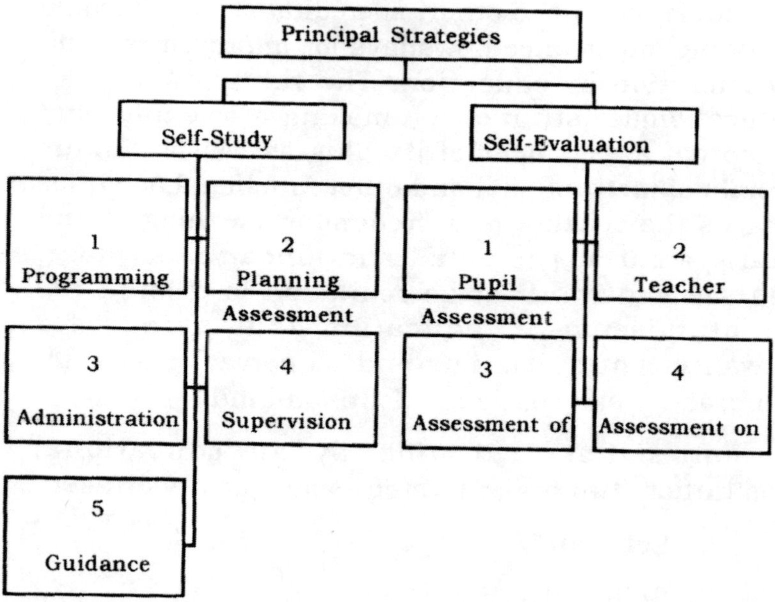

Programming is an essential part of self-study as a strategy for accreditation. The better the organisation of programming, the greater and more effective is the outcome of accreditation through self-study. All this should be ensured by planning that invites four constitutional components:

Table : B

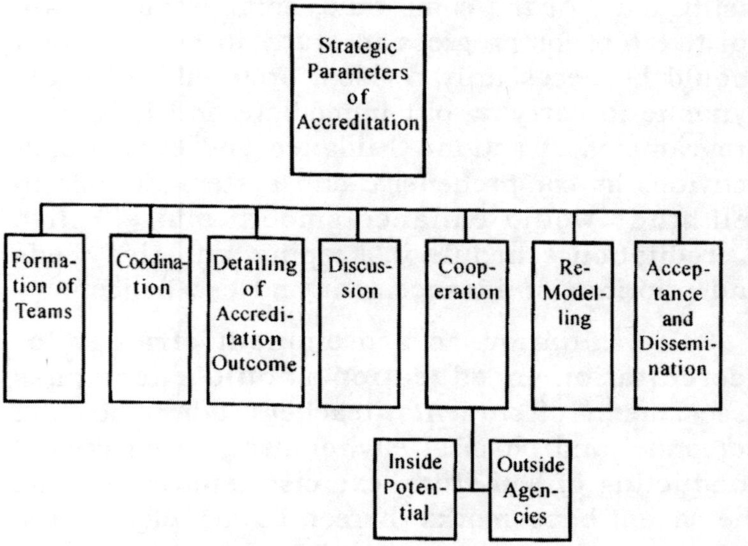

(i) Survey work

(ii) Planning from the low to planning from the high.

(iii) Planning internally and planning externally

(iv) Inviting positive criticism.

(v) Involving everyone for open discussion.

(vi) Selecting salient and pregnant points of deliberations

(vii) Framing additional wings of self-study.

So far as planning for self-study is concerned, the delegation of duties and responsibilities should be made in accordance to a common consensus to be arrived at ensuring the best interest of the learners, teachers and others associated with the institutions. At the same time, administration as a positive tool for progress in study in accreditation should be necessarily revised, oriented and made dynamic in carrying out immediate and long-term programmes of action. Guidance and supervision activities as comprehensive and systematic aids to self-study would enhance smooth and effective accreditation schedule in keeping with the needs and priorities of advancement and excellence.

Self-evaluation as a prominent strategy for accreditation in education should encompass assessments of students, teachers, administration personnel and physical environment. In successful conducting of self-study exercise, and identifying the salient benchmarks thereof, Powar refers to the following:

The various steps to be undertaken by an institution conducting self-study exercises are:

1. Appointment of a self-study co-ordinator and self-study leaders.
2. If considered, necessary arranging for the visit of a representative of the accrediting agency for familiarising the self-study leaders with the purpose and procedure of accreditation, and with the expectations of the accrediting agency.
3. Collection of all required data on students, faculty, administrative staff, organisational structure, physical facilities, academic programmes, and financial resources/status of the institution.

4. Evaluation of data in the light of the institution's mission, goals and objectives. This should bring out the strengths and weaknesses of the institution and identify its opportunities and threats.

— K. B. Powar: *Accreditation in Higher Educaton,* Viva Books Private Limited, New Delhi, 1996.

So far as the strategic parameters of accreditation is concerned, all the components as referred to in Table B should be processed in a very systematic and disciplined way so that there may not be any room for any doubt or discrepancy in regard to the norm and quality of accreditation. At the same time, the following also deserve to be maintained:

(a) The formation of the team for the purpose of accreditation should be free from all narrowness of vision.

(b) The team must act in a conjoint, communicated and judicious way.

(c) The members of the team would be forewarned against any personal interest or temptation.

(d) Absolute co-ordination should be made in undertaking any decision in accreditation.

(e) In co-ordination quality should not be allowed to be jeopardised under any circumstances.

(f) In seeking co-operation both from internal members as well as from outside agencies, a code of conduct should be made as a guideline and all discussions and deliberations should be directed accordingly.

(g) In detailing of accreditation strategies, care should be taken to

(i) Date and time of holding the programme for accreditation.

(ii) Total number of sessions.

(iii) Areas covered for accreditation.

(iv) Discussion papers/literature.

(v) Framing the preamble to discussion.

(vi) Highlighting the salient points of accreditation.

(vii) Re-modelling the programme for accreditation, if necessary.

(viii) Prioritisation of dissemination items.

(ix) Programming of dissemination.

The role of the National Assessment and Accreditation Council (NAAC) in education for assessment and accreditation is undeniably legion. Since its inception in 1994, it has been making a pioneering role in upholding and accelerating quality education as its process of accreditation is greatly contributing to quality culture throughout the country. Its parameters and ends-in-view of activities are distinctly spelt out as follows:

> The NAAC's accreditation process has helped the colleges and universities to know their strengths, weaknesses and opportunities through an informal review. Identification of internal areas of planning and resource allocation was possible because of the accreditation. The self-evaluation, which is an important process in the accreditation, has enhanced collegiality in the campus. The accreditation has provided reliable inputs to funding agencies and governments. A systematic database for performance funding has been provided. The accreditation has helped institutions to initiate innovative and modern methods of pedagogy. It has given a new sense of direction and identity. The accreditation has provided reliable information to various stakeholders on the quality of education offered by the institutions. It has promoted intra-institutional and inter-institutional interactions. The NAAC has undertaken the following activities:
>
> - Encourage the State Governments to take a pro-active role in the accreditation process and help the NAAC to organise seminars, orientation programmes/ discussions, and meeting for principals, teachers, managers,

students for understanding the relevance and advantages of accreditation.

- Establishment of an effective mechanism in every State to monitor the progress of assessment as accreditation.
- Promote new initiatives like credit transfer, student mobility, mutual recognition etc.
- Networking among the accredited institutions in order to promote exchange of 'Best Practices'.
- Formation of Quality Circles for follow up of accreditation outcomes.
- Promoting the concept of lead colleges and cluster of colleges for quality initiatives.
- State wise analysis of accreditation results for policy initiatives.
- Research grants for faculty of accreditation institutions to execute projects.
- Financial support to accredited institutions for conducting seminars/conferences/workshops etc. on quality issues in higher education.
- Developing interval linkages for mutual recognition.

- Collaborating with other national professional bodies for accreditation of specialised subjects.
- NAAC-IGNOU (DEC) joint venture to access Open Universities and CCIs.
- State-Level Coordination Committees for Accreditation.
- National Consultative Committee for Accreditation in different areas.
- Departmental accreditation in Universities and autonomous institutions.
- Providing opportunities for formal interaction with accredited and non-accredited institutions and also with various governmental and non-governmental funding agencies.
- Interaction with other agencies to develop a National Quality Framework.
- NAAC-NCTE joint activity for Self-Appraisal and Accreditation for Teacher Education Institutions.
- CII-NAAC Higher Education summits.

— V. N. Rajasekharan Pillai: "From the Editor's Desk", *NAAC News*, Quarterly Newsletter of the National Assessment and Accredita-tion Council, Bangalore, Vol. III, Issue 3, April 2003, pp. 1-2.

Education crystallised in and through assessment and accreditation is actually addressing dynamism, quality and excellence. As such, evolution of consciousness by means of education of the right kind becomes a natural and spontaneous outcome. Moreover, an all round participation in education for development of the inner world of creativity and positive thinking enshrined with humane sensibilities in course of assessment and accreditation makes education an unending adventure into the world of knowledge and wisdom, edification and appreciation.

The quest for total quality assurance in assessment has already received a green signal from the global world of education. Today's excellence in assessment and accreditation has also brought forth newer challenges for exploring more refined and sophisticated tunings in quality transparency and research avenues in the furtherance of dexterity and penetrating vision.

Why not hope for the best in education and accreditation right from the first decade of the twenty-first century?

5

Re-Thinking Education for All

Education for all as it appears today is more a favourite catch phrase than a thriving reality. It lacks challenge, charm and choice of pinpointed, scientific and practical approach that accommodates a happy and hearty marriage between contemplation and action, promise and perfection. It is as one cannot but admit, more or less pawned to evaluation-shy policies and power-games especially in a pluralistic country like ours where democracy is challenged in and through quality-dwarfed mind-sets.

That enviable education for all has yet remained a dream even after five decades and a half of our national independence necessitates no interpretation statistical or otherwise. Suffice it to say that the picture of literacy for all, leaving aside education for all-round development, is terribly gloomy and almost on the verge of total eclipse without any significant hope of advancement in positive thinking. Who denies that there is even now the appalling difference so categorically remarked by the Education Commission (1964-66) in the very opening chapter, between the high and the low, the rich and the poor, the advantaged and the disadvantaged where education for all is sandwiched in silence and passivity amidst a shameful mockery in the pursuit of learning for enlightened humanity?

Apart from the fact that education to be truly and sincerely for all is even now meant for the limited few, thanks a lot to the legacy carried out deliberately or in the camouflaged form of the colonial system of education, the rampantly breeding ground of opportunism and prioritisation of narrowness standing in the way of a healthy exercise of the fundamental right to education guaranteed by the Indian Constitution is a challenge and choice between darkness and light. A certain positive step to ward off the vulnerable constraints of progress towards education for one and all awaits a concerned, conjoint and communicated endeavour well nursed in continual, disciplined, natural and vibrant approach to learning in freedom and joy.

Admittedly, to be justified to education for all is to be true to the World Declaration on Education for All that emphasises on achievement of 'minimum levels of competence' in the fundamental areas of cognitive skills:

Every person—child, youth and adult—shall be able to benefit from educational opportunities designed to meet their learning needs. These needs comprise both essential learning tools (such as literacy, oral expression, numeracy, and problem solving) and the basic learning content (such as knowledge, skills, values and attitudes) required by human beings to be able to survive, to develop their full capacities, to live and work in dignity, to participate fully in development, to improve the qualities of their lives, to make informed decisions, and to continue learning.

— World Declaration on Education for All, Art. 1, Para 1.

Recalling the 93rd Amendment of the Constitution in Education as a fundamental right, one cannot but admit that there is an inexcusable absence of minimum infra-structural facilities like drinking water, classrooms, teachers, text-books, teaching aids and buildings. Simply toying with sporadic and more or less emotionally surcharged literacy campaign has already prized us with undisturbed slumber in rampant wastage of huge money and manpower.

Meanwhile, the application of advanced technology has sordidly embraced erroneous avenues of education for all in the absence of appropriate surveys, programmes, planning, execution, evaluation and promising remedial measures. Do-it-yourself doping, for instance, of hi-tech sectors has appallingly dragged education to drab utilitarianism leaving harrowing husks in the name of education for quality and human advancement. In fact, with all forms of slovenliness and patchwork in literacy for all, education for values enjoys unchallenged holidays in the top-dressing of vulnerable objectives encapsulated in education for all.

Moreover, a reality-shy strategy of education for all cannot but be a miserable failure to satisfactorily negotiate the aggravating and deepening crisis of unemployment. Who welcomes the really very brilliant products from institutions of education for all? One interested in and devoted to the promotion and dissemination of education for all may recall how an outstanding scholar and teacher of a reputed suburban college of West Bengal, who was a product of Lokasiksha-Sansad under Visva-Bharati, Santiniketan, had to face undesirable problems related to his appointment and recognition of his degree. If correspondence course institutions and open universities in our country at present make an in-depth study of the job involvements of their clientele there might be more unfortunate tales in the context of step-motherly attitude, non-acceptability and recognition of degrees, diplomas, certificates etc. Inaction and frustration have, in the meantime, writ large in the arena of education for all because there is already a very bleak picture of passivity that has staggeringly consolidated the raindrops of education for fall!

Indeed, it is high time to honour and revive Rabindranath Tagore's incomparable and untiring endeavour to make education for all worthwhile in all respects. The unparalleled venture he made in Visva-Bharati in the teeth of all oppositions right back in 1935 to make education for all a thrilling success in associating great scholars in diverse disciplines to write books for the deprived pupils ought to be given due respect and taken up as an emulating incentive for going ahead with newer programmes of advancement of learning. When would formal education on the one hand and informal, distant and non-formal education on the other be tuned in the symphony of oneness that highlights education as a means of exercise and acceleration of excellence notwithstanding avenues diverse and different, rigid or flexible notwithstanding?

A recent phenomenon with persons or clientele under the education for all umbrella calls forth painful stories so far as occupational climate all over India is concerned. It is really undeniable that they somehow eke out their living in low income occupations, if available, as the doors of the higher ones are exclusively meant for the orthodox formal education elites. Under the circumstances, one can easily imagine how social harmony and national integration are being slowly but alarmingly jeopardised in undesirable but perhaps unavoidable social complexes exorbitantly nourished in economic disparities.

Undeniably, the participation of learners in education for all should be carefully analysed and probed at the backdrop of multidimensional socio-economic constraints. In this regard, we may be forewarned with the significant observations of the Ramamurti Commission:

The continued failures since independence to fulfil the Constitutional directive of providing education to all children up to the age of 14 years is a teasing reality. Undoubtedly, this problem qualifies for being ranked as the most fundamental problem of our educational system. It is only in recent years that the nation has come to acknowledge the magnitude of the problem. More than half of all children (and not one-third, as was often claimed for years) and two-thirds of the girls are outside the ambit of education. Whatever hesitation still now exists must now give way to a frank admission of these facts so that an honest analysis of the causes of the problem may begin. The degree of failure is further accentuated in case the children of SC/ST and other educationally backward sections of society. The focus of the various strategies adopted so far to bring all children into schools has been on the factors, which lie within the educational system.

This is equally true of the NPA/POA. The socio-economic and cultural factors have played only a marginal role in educational planning. The approach to universalisation ignores the hard social realities. For instance, according to certain estimates, more than 4.5 crores of children, constituting one-fourth of the school-going age group, are engaged in child labour. Many of these children face brutal work-condition in both the organised and unorganised sectors. The issues of social justice with respect to the educationally backward sections of the society and gender bias rooted in the Indian patriarchal society are some of the other significant factors that have a major bearing upon participation of children in education.

—Committee for Review of National Policy of Education 1986, Final Report, New Delhi, December 1990, *Towards an Enlightened and Humane Society*, pp.134-35.

Education for all is not a mere end-in-view of education as such but a commitment crucial and obligatory, all-time caressing and compulsory:

- First, it must encapsulate the fundamental objectives that bring about a definite healthy, and worthwhile change of mind-sets in social, national and global development.
- Secondly, the right to live and enrichment of human dignity should be given topmost priority in all programmes of action related to education for all.
- Thirdly, work-culture and work ethics concerned with education for all necessitate apposite accommodation and appreciation of values and humane sensibilities in right earnest.

- Fourthly, care should be taken to justify quality and excellence in education for all at every level. Fifthly, no sub-standard education in the name of so-called popularised policy of education for all should be entertained and introduced.

What is primarily needed in organisation of education for all is to admit real-life situation and chalk out well-tailored plans and programmes of action specially suited to prioritised and vulnerable areas of implementation. A major shift in approach should be geared to two-fold strategy of action:

- First, the immediate thrust should cater to the BPL clientele. These below poverty line learners need a special academic climate where the programmes of action are to be clubbed with poverty eradication/alleviation by means of introducing work-oriented education.
- Second, the education of sympathy well co-ordinated with an objective, scientific, fool proof and poignant possibilities of ascent and excellence should be the guiding line towards this direction.

As regards long-term action, care should be taken to achieve the ends-in-view of education for all from all promising perspectives of education for fullness of mankind.

Admittedly, fullness in education for all in terms of educational equity, if not competitiveness, verges on improbability. But, then, education is a challenge any time anywhere. More so is it in the case of the educationally deprived and ignored. Unless there is a continual and sustained quest for the better exploration and efflorescence of the really talented and promising pupils lost in the melee of the educationally backward and deprived sections of the society, education for all would simply be a futile endeavour at building castles of competence and development in the air. In this connection, the invaluable words of the Delors Commission deserves everyone's immediate attention:

> Significantly, the vast and rapid expansion of the education system, and its over-burdening in many countries, have resulted in the inability to attend adequately to the question of educational equity, which calls for providing learning experiences appropriate to the learning needs of students with varying abilities. In the overwhelming ambition to provide education for all, the needs of students with high potential have been neglected and students with differing abilities have been treated equally. As Jefferson once said: 'there is nothing more unequal than equal treatment of unequal people.' Notwithstanding the good intentions of traditional policies, to deprive outstanding students of appropriate educational opportunities is to deprive society of the best human resources that lead towards real and effective development.
>
> —*Learning The Treasure Within*, UNESCO, Paris, 1996, p. 194

As a matter of fact, education for all necessitates a very sound and effective psychological and dynamic parameter where individual differences are judiciously negotiated with a view to accelerating immense possibilities of manifestation of creative and critical consciousness. If education for all remains satisfied with quantitative success as it appears to be so almost everywhere at present, then it cannot but lose much of its desired aims and objectives encompassing acceleration of human development. A time will come—it has actually come—when people from all walks of life will surely look askance at its very importance and justification from the standpoint of its arbitrary, biased, slovenly and dubious role in the name of march towards prosperity and ascent of man.

Education for all also awaits a synchronisation of the exciting patterns of education from manifold perspectives under the umbrella of non-discrimination. Unless this is greatly emphasised, education for all cannot thrive in isolation. As the Platform for Action suggests:

Education is a human right and an essential tool for achieving the goals of equality, development and peace. Non-discriminatory education benefits both girls and boys, and thus ultimately contributes to more equal relationships between women and men. Equality of access to and attainment of educational qualifications is necessary if more women are to become agents of change. Literacy of women is an important key to improving health, nutrition and education in the family and to empowering women to participate in decision-making in the society. Investing in formal and non-formal education and training for girls and women, with its exceptionally high social and economic return, has proved to be one of the best means of achieving sustainable development and economic growth.

—Platform for Action adopted in Beijing in 1995, Paragraph 69

Simultaneously, early childhood education looks forward to revamping in right earnest for promotion of education for global community consciousness at the very onset of entry into the august world of education. This would certainly accentuate and foster participation of parents and guardians and persons from every nook and corner of the country to rise as one man in translating education for all a thrilling reality. As the Report to UNESCO categorically spells out:

> Regrettably, early childhood education is still very poorly developed in most countries of the world, and although in the highly industrial countries most children attend pre-primary school, there is much progress to be made there also. Where a child-development component can be integrated into a multi-purpose community service, very low-cost programmes can be set up. Early childhood education can also be integrated into community education programmes for parents, particularly in developing countries where the high cost of institutional pre-school education makes it available only to the privileged. It is to be hoped that efforts will be launched or continued to extend early childhood learning opportunities all over the world, as part of the push to make universal basic education a reality.
>
> — Report to UNESCO of the International Commission on Education for the Twenty-first Century, UNESCO, 1996, pp.121-22

Indeed, community participation in education for all is yet in its infancy in our country so far as conjoint and communicated contribution to altruistic educational endeavour is concerned. With a little care and caution in close association with sincerity and devotion, such kind of participation may eliminate many constraints and work wonders in the arena of advancement in education for all. As the Commission characteristically points out:

> The success of schooling depends in very large

measure upon the values that communities attach to education. Where education is highly valued and actively sought, the mission and goals of the school are shared and supported by the community. Thus, the increasing focus on the role of local communities needs to be encouraged and supported. Education needs to be seen by the community as applicable to their real-life situations, needs and aspirations. Specific characteristics of life in both rural and urban environments should be taken into account through decisions about the language of instruction and a careful analysis of what needs to be adapted in the curriculum, course content, teacher training and materials.

— Ibid, pp. 122-23.

To be forewarned against our failure to achieve total literacy as early as possible is to be forearmed against undesirable unrest and imbalance between educational objectives in theory and actual success in practice in association with education for the welfare of all. A look at the gloomy picture of enrolment, drop-outs/stop-outs and re-enrolment in elementary education even now compels one to ponder over the significant observation of the National Policy on Education:

Of 100 enrolled in class I, only 25 children reach class VIII. The rest make do with a smattering of illiteracy or add to the mass of illiterates in the country. It must be emphasised that the schools where the majority of children study, whether in towns or in rural areas, are far poorer in facilities, quality and relevance in education. This is one of the reasons why the dropout rates in these schools are staggeringly higher than those in the schools for the elite. Our position in respect of elementary education, even in comparison with the majority of developing countries, is highly unsatisfactory. If adequate provisions are not made even now for school facilities, requisite number of teachers, restructuring of the curricula and methods of teaching, we will be marching into the twenty-first century with an unacceptably large corpus of illiterate people.

— *Challenge of Education: A Policy Perspective*, Ministry of Education, Government of India, New Delhi, 1985, p. 36

Teaching and training of teachers with a view to enhancing and refining education for all necessitate a radical and revolutionary change. In this respect, the prominent areas should be:

(i) Identifying and arresting behaviour problems of learners.

(ii) Cultivating newer trends and techniques of a positive approach to mass education.

(iii) Monitoring every learner's behaviour towards creative and aesthetic thinking.

(iv) Introducing enjoyable activities to ward off vulnerable constraints of advancement of learning in a favourable and satisfactory climate.

(v) Eliminating class-complex through exercise of finer sensibilities and serene vision of life like co-operation, tolerance and universal brotherhood.

(vi) Reducing environmental stress and strain in course of continual and cautious pursuit of learning.

(vii) Caressing and nursing individual differences in meaningful and innovative educational activities.

A comparative approach education for all for cross-cultural evaluation in day-to-day programme of action adds newer nuances to altruism in educational endeavour. This should be given a natural avenue of efflorescence.

Learning to live together in course of learning to create in freedom and joy awaits a warm welcome in every cathedral of education for all. A certain pattern of catholicity of vision in re-structuring policies and priorities in education for all can no longer adorn the waiting list of action. Are we aware of our odyssey towards excellence long overdue?

6

Motivation Education: Setting the Agenda for Quality Acceleration

Education always awaits motivation. It must be specific and concrete, well spelt-out and transparent, methodical and evaluative. Any programme of education bereft of positive motivation cannot but invite indiscipline and ukase as it invariably happens at the primary stage of education where a little bit of carelessness and evasiveness would certainly call forth disaster and doom. The staggering number of stop-outs at this stage in West Bengal as it is revealed in the *National Human Development Report 2001* of the Planning Commission, Government of India, clearly indicates how motivation takes a back seat in the name of so-called advancement in education. While the dropout rates of boys and girls in classes I-V in All India in 1998-99 are 38.23 per cent and 41.34 per cent respectively, in case of West Bengal these are 46.17 per cent and 54.15 per cent respectively. The Report also states that in West Bengal 49.92 per cent children of these classes leave schools without receiving any motivation for education to continue. When such is the plight of motivation received by the children of our country, whither education?

Admittedly, when there is an appalling lack of motivation, education cannot but enjoy unwarranted holidays, thanks to our bungling of public money. The fivefold constraint of motivation education may be categorically identified.

- First, the pupil environment, the greatest source of motivation education, is unfavourable and disruptive.
- Second, ignorance and apathy born and bred out of socio-economic pressures well substantiated by imbalance in standard of living deviates motivation from taking its natural and spontaneous course.
- Third, the teachers associated fail to do justice to motivation in an unusually big and, of course, uncontrolled classroom climate.
- Fourth, books considered to be very important for motivation are hardly available and/or dealt with necessary devotion and diligence, persuasiveness and patience.
- Fifth, students rarely receive any motivation for learning through co-curricular and vibrant activities, which would lead them to learning to love and let others be loved.

Professional competence in motivation education is long overdue in our country. Setting new agendas for motivation acceleration primarily demands nursing and increasing quality from diverse perspectives. To explore newer avenues of quality in motivation education, four factors necessitate immediate attention:

- One, developing pupil specific programmes of motivation to rationalising and fine tuning egocentric wills and aspirations.
- Two, reflecting promising spurts of pupil innovation and quality enhancement in critical thinking.
- Three, stimulating the positive spurts of pupil-endeavour in order to enable them to arrest over-estimation or under-estimation as the case may be under different and challenging situations.
- Four, providing pupils with ample opportunities to be duly rewarded with justified expectations from teachers in quest of excellence in education.

The quest for quality in motivation education should also conform and contribute to the needs and priorities of the immediate society. In fact, human development is always in close communion with whatever is reflected in the present-day social scenario. Care should be taken to see that quality assurance in motivation education encompasses all the segments of the society irrespective of caste, creed, colour etc. so that human development becomes truly national and global in nature and character. As it is significantly remarked:

> The process of development, in every society, should be ideally viewed and asserted in terms of what it does for an average individual. It has to be seen in terms of the benefits and opportunities that it generates for people and how these are eventually distributed—between men and women,

> the well off and deprived and across regions.
>
> — *National Human Development Report 2001*

Training of teachers for quality acceleration and excellence in motivation education needs a look afresh. For this purpose, effective programmes should be chalked out and implemented from six perspectives. First, teachers should undergo training in different components of skills in motivation by means of simulated classroom teachings. Microteaching and mini-teaching programmes in this regard pay very worthy dividends in terms of quality assurance quality proficiency in involvement and appreciation. Second, the methodology of motivation education for quality improvement is to be intensively exercised in tune with pupil expectation and excellence in a favourable climate of sincerity of purpose both in thought and in action within a specific point of time. Three, getting through the syllabus for study by teachers through orientation courses of motivation education would serve the ideal purpose of the different components of quality inputs amongst the teachers under training, Four, the teachers under training would be able to map and consolidate themselves for evolving newer horizons of quality in motivation education including the most challenging ones like will force and striving for goals. Five, ample opportunities in connection with identifying, analysing and evaluating favourable and unfavourable thoughts and beliefs in motivation by means of undergoing foolproof and contextual strategies of qualitative improvement undoubtedly open thrilling avenues of excellence to a remarkable extent. Six, a conjoint and communicated study and research on motivation education and quality improvement amongst teacher trainees and teacher educators contribute a lot to advancement in education in general and that of teacher education in particular.

Education is changing. This is more so because strategies are changing. Sticking to chalk and talk strategy of teaching for pupil motivation is fast becoming a matter of yore yielding practically no purpose. To build socio-emotional skills systematically by means of motivation education calls forth a computer savvy strategy of quality consciousness where access to global informatics side by side with a subjective approach to focus instruction and evaluation makes education more interesting, meaningful, relevant and purposeful. Thus a landmark success in exploring better strategies in motivation becomes not only possible but also significant in achieving excellence in education.

7

Reviewing Examinations

Are examinations a blessing or a curse? Are they a device or a tool for peril or progress? The questions are ripe now and much mischief has already been afoot. The sordid tales of committing suicides, utter desolation and disappointment amongst young learners especially in secondary and under-graduate levels are nowadays regular features in mass media and other types of informatics. It is a matter of grave concern no doubt that reviews and re-examinations fail to satisfy the hapless lots who seek justice somehow or other denied or ignored. The demands for a photocopy of every answer script may appear to someone silly or redundant but this might appease or console the aching hearts of at least sentimental candidates who have failed to secure desirable dividends in the form of marks.

Admittedly, the ills of examinations breed rampantly in marks and marks. Perhaps no remark is so realistic and prominent but at the same time sadly missing that examinations are nothing but a tool and these should not be given so much emphasis because there are other tools like interviews, self-evaluation etc., which are no mean ones for apposite assessments in learning. But who cares? We are yet to bring about a much-needed revolution in the existing much used-up pen-paper-pencil tests. Whither examinations? Whither education?

The history of examination reforms in India presents us with startling facts about our failures in education at different levels on diverse points. As the Ramamurti Commission elucidates:

> Examination reform has been a subject of almost consistent consideration by various Committees and Commissions appointed by the Government of India from time to time. The justification for examination reforms arises from academic considerations. Examinations along with teaching and learning, in fact, constitute the trinity of functions in the educational process. Examinations over the years have tended to be an instrument for testing memory. Learning has become a rather mechanical process of acquiring skills and teaching has been largely a process of coaching for examinations. The relationship between examinations and standards of teaching and learning are intimate. Improvement in any one of these aspects results in improvement of other aspects as well. Therefore, the objective of examination reform is to make it an instrument of good education.

The Indian University Commission (1902) observed that the teaching in Indian education stood subordinated to examination and not examination to teaching. The Hartog Committee(1929 deprecated academic bias of examinations at the school level, geared as they were to the needs of the majority who did not have access to the university system and were to enter life. Similar criticism was voiced by the Sargent Plan 1944. the Radhakrishnan Commission (1948) pointed out that examination reform was a matter of very high priority in education reform as a whole. The Mudaliar Commission (1952-53) made elaborate recommendations on examination reform and called for reduction in the number of external examinations, conduct of objective tests, assessment of attainments of the students through a proper system of school records, weightage for in-school tests, symbolic rather than numerical marking for purposes of evaluation and grading etc. the Education Commission (1964-66) considered the question of examination reform at all stages of education and called for evaluation being construed as a means to assess learner development on an objective basis. The CABE Committee on Examination Reform (1970) also made wide-ranging recommendations. The National Policy on Education, 1986 also

> considered examinations as a means for improvement of quality of education. Specifically, it called for removal of subjectivity in examinations, de-emphasis of memorisation, continual and comprehensive internal evaluation of scholastic and non-scholastic achievements of students, improvement in the conduct of examinations, introduction of concomitant changes in instructional material and methodology, introduction of the semester system from the secondary stage in a phased manner and use of grades in the place of marks. The Programme of Action (PCA) suggested several specific short-term and long-term measures for carrying out examination reform at the school level as well as the university level.
>
> —*Towards an Enlightened and Humane Society,* "Report of the Committee for Review of National Policy on Education 1986", New Delhi, 1990, p. 290.

Apart from the fact that examinations in most cases are failing to do justice to both examinees and examiners in many respects and diverse dimensions, we are yet to gear our evaluation processes towards significantly negotiating the ends-in-view of assessment that really care for learning the treasure within so characteristically advocated by the Delors Report to UNESCO of the International Commission on Education in the Twenty-first Century:

> People today have a dizzying feeling of being torn between a globalization whose manifestations they can see and sometimes have to endure, and their search for roots, reference points and a sense of belonging.
>
> Education has to face up to this problem now more than ever as a world society struggles painfully to be born: education is at the heart of both personal and community development; its mission is to enable each of us, without exception, to develop all our talents to the full and to realize our creative potential, including responsibility for our own lives and achievement of our personal aims.
>
> —*Learning: The Treasure Within*, UNESCO, 1996, pp. 18-19.

A real examination embracing evaluation of exposition of treasure within is yet to be launched in all sincerity of purpose.

Examinations at any stage for evaluation in the right perspective as above do encapsulate the four-fold factor viz., the extent and quality of teaching, a fool-proof evaluation-prone syllabus for every subject, the feedback pattern at every step of learning, evaluation and analysis of evaluation, and the role of efficient teachers and administrators who are always alert in restoring discipline at all costs. Are examinations today paying heed to this fact?

From the teaching point of view, examinations demand a fair world of questions — probing, pin pointed, purposeful, meaningful and relevant. Again, examinations do demand a prior arena of natural habitations entailing practice and performance well synchronised, challenging and thrilling to the clientele. This is no mean task. If the joy of learning and that of evaluation are not well clubbed to crystallise examinations, the purpose of the latter is terribly defeated.

Educational administrators also play a very vital role in the success of examinations. Examinees rightly demand justice to their evaluation reports. All successes and failures in examinations are equally important and therefore administration in this regard should cater to all queries and doubts to be dispelled by appropriate and loving measures where the harmony of relationship between administration and examination is never shattered in slightest possible strained and disastrous relationships. Indeed, a cordial relationship between the two enhances education of the right mind in right order and right dimensions.

Our societal moorings and ethos on examinations await a sea change. When would we do away with committing the Himalayan blunder that success in examinations on the part of a learner is the be-all and end-all of education? A further examination with many more divergent pullouts calls forth our attention. Moreover, eyeing examinations as the only passport to attaining fullness of man is a social evil. Why not arrest this evil right now?

Indeed, the contemporary educational scenario is terribly plagued by the erroneous examination system. As it is significantly observed:

> No description of the contemporary educational scenario can be complete

> without a reference to the examination system since it decides, not only the fate of students, but also the content, orientation as well as the quality of education at all levels. Apart from evaluating examinees on the basis of rote learning and memorising, their annual periodicity creates an environment in which students tend to while away their time for most part of the year and gear themselves to work for the last three or four months. For obvious reasons, lack of continuity in application results in the building up of unbearable pressures at the end of the year which find expression in boycott of examinations, leakage of question papers, mass-copying, payment of bribes to evaluators and other unethical practices. Consequently, degrees and grades do not generally command credibility as a whole with the public as well employers in the public and private sectors and the whole process of higher education has become warped, disoriented and dysfunctional, producing a large number of unemployed young men and women.
>
> —*Challenge of Education: A Policy Perspective,*
>
> Ministry of Education, Government of India, August 1965, p. 9

Prior to making any probe into the present examination system, one cannot but negotiate with the following questions:

(a) Is it an integral part of the pupil assessment?

(b) Is it a positive contributing component to better learning and teaching?

(c) Does it really play a vital role in the qualitative improvement of education as a whole?

(d) Is it interesting to the learner and to the teacher as well?

(e) Is it free from errors?

(f) Does it allow or affirm malpractice or unfair means?

(g) Is the society learning or otherwise satisfied with pupil performance or holding examinations in a slovenly manner?

(h) Is it detrimental to intellectual and emotional developments of learners?

(i) Does it aggravate pupils' psychological and socio-aesthetic imbalance?

(j) Does it act as a deterrent to pupils' all round normal growth and development?

(k) Does it hamper normal dealings with daily courses of learning and teaching?

(l) Is it simply wastage of time and energy of learners as well as teachers?

(m) Does it supplement to making an endless adventure into the world of education?

One can go on adding hundreds of queries on the examination system because it is so much prone to lopsidedness that in the absence of a little bit of alertness and sincerity and, above all, discipline, the whole system miserably fails and affects the minds of both the pupils and the teachers and the others concerned with worthwhile education. As a matter of fact, educational experts and planners of education are seriously thinking about setting alternative agendas for bringing about qualitative changes in the present system of examinations formulated and conducted by the boards of examinations at different educational institutions in India.[1]

Newer strategies for examination reforms have been introduced. Facilities for learner participation in the reform itself have yielded positive results. A package deal with reforms on the examinations held at different levels have been well responded. Individual differences among students meant for pupil evaluation through examinations have been carefully addressed.

In addition to the above, the credit system, semester system, entrance test, internal assessment, and other newer policies on examination reforms are also introduced. Even more radical and pro-active strategies for examination reforms are being introduced in self-appraisal and accreditation programmes of activities. The package for reforms in the examination system as suggested by the Ramamurti Commission may now serve as a distinctive guideline for positive onward programme of activities:

(i) The question of examination reform should be construed as a package of all the following factors:

- Introduction of semester system.
- Continuous internal evaluation; and maintenance of integrity of such evaluation (and examination in whatever form and scale they may be conducted); within the same classes, in primary stage, disaggregated evaluation of groups of students to cater to individual differences.
- Teachers playing the key role, the principle being "He or she who teaches shall lay down the syllabus and also evaluate".
- Facilities for students to move from one stage of education to another by appearing in entrance tests.
- Facilities for students to have the freedom of choice of modules rather than whole course packages.
- Provisions for credit accumulation by students and facilities for transfer of grade from one institution to the another; facilities of multiple entry and exit for students which in effect facilitates *opening up* and *non-formalising* the school system.

It is this *package* as a whole which should be brought under implementation and not merely individual elements, that too in a piecemeal or ad-hoc fashion.

—*Towards an Enlightened and Humane Society*, Report of the Committee for Review of National Policy on Education (NPE) 1986, New Delhi, 1990, p. 296.

Meanwhile, scams in conducting examinations, biased reviews and re-examinations, dangerous internal assessments, total chaos and indiscipline in the examination centres, sharking of responsibilities by invigilators, centre-superintendents, underhand practices by other examination personnel—all have already made massacres in examinations so much so that good sense and sensibilities absolutely desirable for examinations to be perfectly performed are very much jeopardised and defeated under appalling circumstances. About malpractices of diverse kinds that one come across even after taking many precautionary measures at the time holding examinations are:

- Putting symbols on answer scripts or foreign matters—paper strips, thread ends, stickers etc.—for advantageous identification.
- Taking assistance of teachers/ invigilators at the cost of other examinees.
- Maintaining underhand nexus with outside agencies under money or muscle power.

- Putting an abrupt halt in the smooth function of examination programmes by creating unabated disturbance in examination centres,
- Raising delicate issues not even slightly related to examinations in order to disrupt examination schedules.
- Destroying answer books and additional sheets or slipping away from the examination centres with answer scripts.
- Manhandling invigilators as and when desired for cancelling examinations.
- Erroneous question papers due to absence of reliable and valid moderation.
- Biased handling of discipline, punctuality and instructions for appropriate conduct of examination.
- Careless invigilation.
- Encroachment of undesirable persons in the centres of examinations.

To eliminate the loopholes of the examination reforms, Examination Reforms Commission with the following terms of reference has been suggested:

(i) Review of the status of examination reforms from time to time.

(ii) Phasing of examination reforms, indicating time-frame within which, and levels at which, the reforms are to be effected.

(iii) Introduction of fair and objective systems of grading/scaling.

(iv) Laying down norms of continuous comprehensive internal evaluation and suggesting safeguards against abuse of this evaluation system.

(v) Advising on minimum levels of learning to go with internal evaluation system.

(vi) Laying down modalities foe semesterisation and modularisation.

(vii) Advising on iter-institutional linkages to secure comparable standards.

(viii) Teacher orientation for successful implementation of examination reforms.

—*Ibid, p. 297*

Admittedly, any programme of implementation of examination reform should be preceded by a forewarning that the schools must not be treated as conveyer belts for turning out pupils for higher education in colleges and universities but as a hallowed centre of growth and development of all-round personality. The first point to remember in reviewing examinations starts with this premise and promise as well that no examination becomes meaningful and worthwhile unless it is rooted to the learning of all and not of the few in the society who are blessed with an ideal learning environment and opportunity.

When would we justify ourselves to the statement: Reviewers, review education realistically and meaningfully not in principles alone but with practice as well?

The following table shows the status of implementation of examination reforms at the school level.

Sl.	*Steps for Examination Reforms*	*Boards/ States which have Introduced Reform*
1.	Development of policy statement (design) for each question paper.	Andhra Pradesh, Assam, Gujarat, Kerala, Maharashtra, Punjab, Rajasthan, CISCE, J&K, M.P., Manipur, CBSE, Haryana, Tripura, Karnataka, Goa, U.P., West Bengal
2.	Appointment of paper-setters from among those trained in evaluation.	Andhra Pradesh, Gujarat, Kerala, Maharastra, Orissa, Rajasthan, CISCE, J&K, M.P., Manipur, Tamil Nadu, Haryana, Goa, U. P. West Bengal.
3.	Appointment of panels of paper-setters for each question paper.	Andhra Pradesh, Assam, Kerala, Gujarat, Maharashtra, Rajasthan, CISCE, Tripura, Goa, U. P.
4.	Allocation of definite proportionate percentages of marks in question papers for testing different abilities.	Andhra Pradesh, Assam, Gujarat, Maharashtra, Kerala, Rajasthan, CISCE, J & K, M. P., CBSE, Haryana, Manipur, Tripura, Karnatak, Goa, U. P.
5.	Ensuring an effective coverage of the syllabus through the question papers.	Andhra Pradesh, Assam, Gujarat, Kerala, Maharashtra, Rajasthan, CISCE, CBSE, J & K, Manipur, M. P., Haryana, Goa, U.P.
6.	Introduction of specific pin-pointed questions in the question paper.	Andhra Pradesh, Assam, Gujarat, Karnataka, Kerala, Maharashtra, CISCE, CBSE, Haryana, Tripura, Goa, U. P., West Bengal
7.	Inclusion of short-answer questions in the question papers, besides the essay-type ones.	Andhra Pradesh, Assam, Gujarat, Karnataka, Kerala, Maharashtra, Manipur, Orissa, Punjab, Rajasthan, Tamil Nadu, CISCE, CBSE, Haryana, Tripura, Goa, U.P., West Bengal
8.	Introduction of objective type questions (multiple choice) in the question papers.	Andhra Pradesh, Gujarat, Karnataka, Kerala, Maharashtra, Manipur, Orissa, Punjab, Rajasthan,

	Tamil Nadu, CISCE, Tripura, Goa, U. P.
9. Use of question banks for setting question papers.	Gujarat, Rajasthan, CISCE, Goa, Bihar, CBSE, Haryana, West Bengal.
10. Abolition of overall options in the question papers.	Andhra Pradesh, Assam, Gujarat, Karnataka, Kerala, Orissa, Rajasthan, CBSE, U. P.
11. Development of marking scheme along with each question paper by the setter himself.	Assam, Gujarat, Karnataka, Kerala, Punjab, Rajasthan, CISCE, CBSE, U. P., Goa, Maharashtra, West Bengal.
12. Division of question papers into separate sections for fixed response and free response questions with fixed separate limit.	Andhra Pradesh, Gujarat, Kerala, Karnataka, Punjab, Rajasthan, Tamil Nadu, CISCE.
13. Introduction of centralized spot evaluation of scripts.	Andhra Pradesh, Gujarat, Kerala, Karnataka, Maharashtra, Rajasthan, CISCE, CBSE, U.P.
14. Introduction of mechanical processing of examination results.	Andhra Pradesh, Assam, Gujarat, Karnataka, Kerala, Tamil Nadu, CISCE, CBSE, Tripura, Goa, U. P.
15. Scaling of subject-wise results for making them comparable.	Gujarat, Kerala, CISCE.
16. Allowing students to clear the examination in parts.	Andhra Pradesh, Karnataka, Kerala, Rajasthan, Punjab, CBSE.
17. Permitting students to improve their grades by appearing at subsequent examination.	Andhra Pradesh, Karnataka, Kerala, Rajasthan, Punjab, CBSE.
18. Reckoning both the product and performance in evaluation of practical work in science subject.	Assam, Gujarat, Kerala, Punjab, Maharashtra, Rajasthan, CISCE, Tripura, CBSE, Goa, U. P.
19. Incorporation of both academic and non-academic areas of pupil growth in the scheme subject.	Rajasthan, Tamil Nadu.

20. Issue of separate certificate of internal assessment along with that of external examination.	Rajasthan.
21. Analysis of question papers in details as feedback for paper-setters.	Rajasthan.
22. Analysis of answer-scripts of the examination locating common errors, correlation in score and functional value of item, etc.	Rajasthan.
23. Autonomy to schools in curriculum teaching, text-books and evaluation etc.	Rajasthan.

8

Teacher Education at Crossroads

Teacher education is one of the most complicated and burning issues of education today. Prior to independence, our country was almost deprived of any satisfactory and promising avenues of excellence in the education of teachers. Of course, there were a few institutions run by private organizations and missionaries who weighed their balance of education primarily to serve their very specific purpose not altogether directed towards all-round progress of the then yoked nation encompassing enrichment in all branches of knowledge in general and dissemination of education of the masses and indigenous education in particular. Apart from the fact that education in the pre-independence era was meant not for all but for the limited few to serve vested interests in the best possible ways, the scenario in the post-independent India is, let us frankly admit, more or less dismal. We are yet to satisfactorily negotiate the major constraints of teacher education and give a remarkable facelift so much so that with sustained and sincere involvements of dedicated and devoted teaching personnel the country gets a vibrant thrust in advancement of learning in general and quality in teacher education in particular.

Admittedly, teacher education today is burdened with countless constraints some of which may be prominently identified as follows:

(a) There is practically no uniform pattern of curriculum for teacher education throughout the country.

(b) Innumerable ill-stratified and slovenly earmarked courses of teacher education hardly comply with the minimum expectations of fulfilment and excellence in ends-in-view of education.

(c) Better quality of teaching in any discipline due to continual absence of better teacher preparation and training is even now a harsh but undeniable reality.

(d) Absence of accreditation and apposite evaluation of teacher educators have been unendingly damaging the challenging prospects and priorities of ascent and excellence.

(e) Lack of provision for making teacher education well concerned with and contributory to other branches of knowledge and erudition in order to sincerely cultivate a steadfast inter-disciplinary approach is paving ample avenues of sub-standard and low-key education.

(f) Absence of a judicious approach to revitalize the ethos and moorings, culture and heritage of our country in order to sensitise the spirit of national cohesion by means of the education of teachers of the right kind and right mind is making our teacher education programmes of activities ineffective.

(g) That the country's diverse and different strategies for improving and accelerating quality in teacher education necessitates an immediate revamping through association and incorporation, wherever and wherever necessary, of global teacher education programmes is yet to be given appropriate emphasis.

Undeniably, teacher education in India looks forward to re-thinking, re-designing and re-evaluating aesthetics in teaching. How to be alive with teaching for cultivation and dissemination of good sense and sensibilities, values, discipline and, above all, self-respect and self-advancement for the benefit of one and all are, indeed, the fundamental avenues of negotiating the appalling shortcomings of teacher education.

Moreover, the eternal spirit of education in highlighting service with untiring devotion and diligence — *pranipatena pariprasnena sevaya* – needs an exercise anew and afresh. The exercise of the age-old Indian aesthetic spirit of simplicity and stick-to-itiveness to truth, beauty, goodness, love, benevolence, patience and many other socio-aesthetic traits of personality development should be pointers to permanent progress in teacher education. That a teacher today is more than a nation builder and continually contributes to re-shaping and re-establishing a brave new world of global .teaching and personality efflorescence necessitates a new beginning with all care and caution, involvement and perseverance.

The yawning gaps between contemplation and action, theoretical foundation and practical implementation have no alternative but to call forth the service of an apex institution for teacher improvement and teacher control. Since its inception as a statutory body of the Government of India, the National Council for Teacher Education (NCTE) is assigned with the uphill task of doing away with manifold ukase in teacher education.

Notwithstanding the fact that education is a state subject, the primary constraints of teacher education are worse confounded in spelling out a viable, conjoint and communicated programme of activities well suited to the needs and priorities of advancement of teacher education in every nook and corner of India. There is an urgent necessity of action specially for the purpose of accelerating sandwiched and/or bridge courses of teacher training by setting up new agenda of teacher preparation where the contents. should encompass the following:

I. Course content—matter and stylistics,

II. Value interpretation/assessment,

III. Comparative and contrastive proneness specially in relation to education as a multi-disciplinary synchronizer,

IV. Embracing and actualising education as a science in the generic sense of the term thereby widening and nurturing the scope

> of education as economics education, mathematics education, management education and so on with a vigorous endeavour at updating teacher education to the immediate and likely to be felt needs of the country and the world at large. Truly, teacher education cannot but welcome the diverse prospects and praxes of teacher enrichment by means of widening the horizon of teacher accountability and teacher efficiency.

The crises of good teaching throughout the world are legion and challenging. India, too, is confronted with countless and complex constraints in teacher education. Already, there is a mushrooming of sub-standard teacher clientele who have made education for effective teaching worse confounded with downsizing education as a cheap commodity for devotion-shy bargain. With a negative role of mass awareness as the ace card of profiteering and fulfilling petty interests, there are, of course, vulnerable agencies of education for teachers who make brisk business in mortgaging the so-called teacher educators who have nothing to do in a vicious circle of education for teaching. The confused world of teacher education nowadays badly calls forth a supersonic jolt by means of worthwhile evolution in teaching and training for excellence of teachers in every discipline.

Teacher education is not an isolated activity. It rightly deserves the cooperation of all interested in the promotion of education. It is heartening to note in this connection that Rabindranath Tagore, a teacher educator *par excellence*, looked upon and extensively made experiments on teaching not only in general disciplines but also in special areas of learning namely, agriculture, poultry, woodcraft, weaving, ceramics, banking, boutique and leather work, dairy etc. in order to make education and work wedded to each other and contributing to an inseparable and harmonious way of life. It is also noteworthy in this connection that in response to the urgent needs of the then poverty stricken and ill educated people of India, he sent his son Rathindranath to USA to undergo training in agriculture and utilize the latest scientific and technical know-how to bring about a radical and revolutionary change in training and education in teaching rural masses. His Sriniketan, the abode of plenty as he endearingly christens it, still upholds some of the essentials of teaching for rural reconstruction. As a matter of fact, Tagore alone gave an altogether new line of illuminating and positive direction in the arena of education for effective teaching which drew the attention of no less a celebrated personality than L. K. Elmhirst who sincerely associated himself with the Tagorean teaching and training assignments, loved to write a *chasa* — a ploughman—within parenthesis after putting his signature every time everywhere and paid his homage to Tagore in his excellent book *The Poet and the Ploughman.* When comes such a pulsating teacher educator?

Apart from the fact that teacher education is a consolidated activity, Tagore, himself an incomparable and unparalleled teacher educator, always harped on teaching as a joyous, creative, soulful, vibrant and living activity. Not education as a parrot's training but as a perennial fountain of freedom and joy was the core of his teaching learning process. Which is why he denounced the colonial, age-old and damaging system of education for apathy where the breeding germs of cramming, marks -oriented and erroneous examination-happy strategies of teaching and learning have run riots in rampant ways, and strongly advocated for cultivation of the education of sympathy and creative and aesthetic sensibility.

Undeniably, teacher education till now is not desirably and adequately responsive to Tagore's ideas and ideals of teaching for cultivation of living education. His own vigorous involvement in writing books for the neo-literates and adult learners on science and astronomy besides other branches of learning and engaging illustrious teachers, scholars and scientists like Prasanta Chandra Mahalanobish, Jagadish Chandra Bose, U. N. Brahmachari and others to write books for the non-schooling learners and neo-literates even now await a heartening and sincere response from all interested in education for all and education for fullness. Let our class-rooms for teaching be blessed with an open air ambience where the relationship between the teacher and the taught be based as Tagore translated into reality in his own educational institutions at Visva-Bharati, on the spirit of unending efflorescence of the joyous and innovative quest for Truth in order to translate the inherent force of *anandarupamamritang yadvibhati.* Let the dynamics of teacher education get a grateful go in translating advancement of education for nobler excellence and spirituality of mankind.

Teacher education is yet to track many more miles in our country in doing justice to the multi-dimensional world of pupil-creativity and teaching awareness to rise up to a minimum expectation of pupil-effulgence in accordance with individual creative talent and critical ingenuity. As a matter of fact, the teacher cannot but himself/herself be creative and critical for advancement of learners' spirit of creativity. The ordinary traditional chalk-talk strategy of teaching simply relegates the exercise of pupil-creativity to the background. This also deprives the earnest teacher from having an easy and spontaneous access to the world of newer thoughts and concepts, priorities and promises pregnant with endless possibilities of creative fulfilment. Who denies that in our present day aims and objectives of teacher education very little has been referred to and exercised to ward off the constraints of teacher-learners' world of creativity? The adventure of the creative thrust in the day-to-day teaching-learning process beckons us and it is undoubtedly one of the greatest adventures of all educational experimentations.

Teaching as everyone admits, is a very challenging and complex activity. Unless one delves deep into the world of teaching and learning at the same time, keeping an alert eye on the teaching learning trends and tendencies particularly related to teacher-pupil poignance of thought and action, the whole world of teaching and learning suffers from utter frustration and disappointment. Practically, teaching becomes dull and drab, mechanical and artificial by being wedded to crazy utilitarianism. Hence, the importance of microteaching to bring about a positive, effective, reliable, realistic and satisfactory change for improvement of teaching.

Despite the fact that it is one of the most popular strategies adopted in teacher education and teacher preparation in course of regular and disciplined exercise and observation of teaching skills under simulated class-room situations, it somehow or other invites ambiguities and confusions in spelling out finer points of differences among specific skills like appreciation, attitude, interest etc. and more often than not fails to do justice to some of the intricate issues related to the teaching of language and literature in particular.

Moreover, there is a lot of difference between microteaching and macro teaching, and the twain hardly encounter cordially in the backdrop of teacher-learner ratio-free abnormal classroom situations. Therefore, what the earnest teacher wholeheartedly expects from learners by undergoing strenuous exercise of microteaching ends in a smoke in the live demonstrations of teaching at a macro classroom atmosphere.

Bearing in mind the ample limitations of microteaching as above, one cannot, however, ignore the fact that in teacher education it plays a very significant and effective role in bringing about a major change in teaching for quality and efficiency. In fact, it serves as an enviable and energetic stimulant to launching macro classroom teaching practice programmes. It also enables every teacher-learner to go ahead in creditably negotiating everyday lessons to be taught at different classes on different subjects. The lessons thus delivered as a follow-up of microteaching practice bear characteristic stamps of improvement and excellence specially in exercising some essential and vulnerable skills of teaching.

Unfortunately, teaching in secondary schools are now bereft of these major advantages of the exercise of skills scientifically due to lack of interest and gradual erosion of this very vital strategy of microteaching. When would we realize, re-affirm and synchronize between micro and macro teaching in teacher education?

Teacher education in India has undergone a remarkable change by means of implementing effective strategies for improvement of teaching. The role of the NCTE as an apex national statutory body during the last five years has significantly contributed to a certain sense of positive awareness in sensitising delicate issues in teacher preparation and promotion of quality in teaching. Apart from the fact that the country is yet to registrar and assure zero percent illiteracy, many ticklish issues pertaining to teaching environs, community consciousness, institutional constraints, anomalies in teacher appointments, absence of desirable standards in teaching, imbalance in teacher-pupil ratio, aggravating and ominous pressures from vested interests etc. pose penetrating ukase in arena of teacher education.

The role of the teacher today as a true representative of an enlightened and humane global society has become more significant due to continual knowledge explosion and changing needs and priorities. Today's teacher is not merely a taskmaster of certain fixed assignments dealing with cultivation and dissemination of knowledge items or experiences but he/she ought to respond to the greater and more practical needs that shape and reshape humans in keeping with the evolutionary process of education. As the Delors Commission appositely suggests:

> The teacher's task is not confined simply to transmitting information or

even knowledge; it also entails presenting that knowledge in the form of a statement of problems within a certain context and putting the problems into perspectives, so that the learners can link their solutions to broader issues. The teacher-pupil relationship aims at the full development of the pupil's personality with emphasis on self-reliance; from this point of view of the authority vested in teachers is always paradoxical, since it is not based on assertion of their power but on the pre-recognition of the legitimacy of knowledge. This function of the teacher as a figure of authority will probably evolve, yet it remains as a source of the answers to questions raised by the pupils about the world and as a key pre-requisite for the full success of the learning process. Besides, it is becoming increasingly necessary in modern societies for teaching to help form individual judgement and a sense of individual responsibility, so as to enable pupil to develop the ability to foresee change and to adjust to them, in other words to continue learning throughout their lives. It is through working under and through dialogue with the teacher that a pupil's critical faculty is helped to develop.

— *Learning: The Treasure Within*, Report to UNESCO of the International

Commission on Education for the Twenty-first Century, 1996, p. 145

The teacher today ought to undergo the right training for the right purpose on nation building. Teacher education ought to prepare teacher educators who cannot but take the arduous task of how to prepare in-service and pre-service teachers to fulfil the mission of the role of the teacher as indicated above. Admittedly, ours is a country, which definitely responds to education of the best kind and of the best mind to contribute to creating best and nursing the best citizens of tomorrow. With the rich possibilities of information technology, teacher education ought to consider incorporation of the different knowledge items dealing with the world of information technology. Broader canvases of information well synchronised with education for creative and critical consciousness will certainly lead to evolution in education for teaching and learning not only suited to the needs and possibilities of the twenty-first century but also to many more centuries to come. That knowledge thus cultivated not only grows but also expands keeping in view the importance of eschewing the stylistics of teaching and learning is a fact to be translated into reality by means of making a bond between information technology and education for growth and development of personality.

Accordingly, the syllabus of teacher education necessitates reshuffling in many directions:

- Firstly, old fashioned, obsolete and backdated items of teaching and learning should be appropriately identified and deleted.
- Secondly, incorporation of matters related to real

life situations should come under the purview of teaching and learning.

- Thirdly, a comparative and contrastive approach to teaching and learning should form the very basis of advancement in teacher education.
- Fourthly, for worthwhile transmission of strategies of teaching, teacher exchange programmes should be introduced with care, caution and spontaneity.
- Fifthly, envious incentives for promising and proficient teachers and teacher educators should be regularly provided.

If it is true that teachers best identify and familiarize educational institutions, it is also equally, if not more, true that teacher educators best identify and familiarize teachers. The quality of teaching, therefore, depends on that of teacher educators. Unfortunately, teacher educators, let us frankly admit, fail more or less to do justice to quality in teaching teachers.

Indeed, one cannot help admitting the fact that in many teachers' training institutions of our country very few teacher educators are justified with the minimum required essential qualifications as stipulated by the UGC and the teachers they teach are found to be as qualified as they are. Naturally, they suffer from a complex affecting their teaching assignments. Besides, poor and substandard teaching so imparted makes a very colossal damage in the altar of teacher education.

The importance of the quality of teacher education has never been so prominently felt as it is right now. Poorly trained and motivated teachers can hardly respond to imparting teaching children and adult learners best suited to their socio-economic environs, their individual creative and aesthetic consciousness notwithstanding. Truly, teacher education programmes should be reviewed specially at the primary stage of education so that teachers of primary or basic schools undergo purposeful and vigorous training in negotiating the challenging needs of the country's long standing mission of education for all. The Commission significantly suggests:

> The importance of the quality of teaching, and therefore of teachers cannot be overemphasized. It is at an early stage of basic education that the principal attitudes toward learning as well as the self-image of the learner are formed. The role of the teacher at this stage is crucial. The greater the handicaps, the children coming to school have to overcome — in terms of poverty, difficult social environment or physical; impairments – the greater the demands on the teacher. He or she to be effective must draw upon a broad range of teaching skills as well as on the human qualities empathy, patience and humility as a complement to authority. When a child's or adult's first teacher is poorly trained and poorly motivated, the very foundations on which all subsequent learning will be built will be unsound. The Commission feels that reasserting the importance of the teachers in basic education and improving teachers' qualifications are tasks to which all governments must address themselves. The measures

> needed to recruit future teachers from among the most motivated students, improve their training and encourage the best among them to take on the most difficult posts need to be determined in relation to the specific circumstances of each country.
>
> — Report to UNESCO of the International Commission on Education for the Twenty-first Century, p. 146

Investment of the human talent in teacher education by means of enrichment of teaching skills and revitalising the community spirit would certainly contribute a lot to the advancement of teacher education. Undoubtedly, we will have to shoulder greater duties and responsibilities and work wholeheartedly for a better and enlightened community of teacher educators who are sincerely devoted to prioritise areas of research in teaching at the various stages of education for teaching.

Are we prepared?

9

Tuning the School Climate

Academic reforms are very important for improvement in school education. None denies that education at the school stage forms the very foundation of higher learning. The basic deficiencies at this stage damage all finer visions and prospects of quality education. The recent trend of giving a face-lift to school education in West Bengal is more dramatic than scientific, more elusive than pragmatic. As a matter of fact, secondary education has been undergoing utter ukase for more than two decades, thanks to appalling indifference to the primary needs and priorities of excellence in pupil-learning and pupil-achievement. What with changes in the syllabus-pattern specially in case of English as a second language or with the latest endeavour to arrest private tuition by teachers and curtailing holidays in order to explore more teaching-learning hours, the present scenario of secondary schools is a sordid tale of top-dressing with blunt and baffled weapons in the name of educational planning, administration and supervision.

Admittedly, aimless and perfunctory ends-in-view of educational planning, administration and supervision writ large in school education in particular have gravely crippled all good intentions and rejuvenation in both rural and urban centres of learning. A casual visit to any secondary school, barring a very few ones, in West Bengal will undeniably present one with the following facts:

(a) There is hardly any favourable physical climate for accelerating desirable and ideal teaching-learning norms, quality and excellence. Unsafe and dingy classrooms, irregular supply of pure drinking water, poor sanitation and academic environ, to mention a few constraints, stand in the way of worthwhile education.

(b) So far as the aesthetic climate of every seat of learning is concerned, the less said the better. Classrooms adorned with portraits of celebrated personalities, display of school magazines enriched with selected articles, pictures, drawings, paintings and so on, nurturing flower gardens and equipping school play-grounds are, let us frankly admit, few and far between.

Open plans as an essential component of holding open-air classes blessed with a pleasing and aesthetic classroom environment are rarely encountered. How, then, is it possible to be natural with Nature and human with humane sensibilities so poignantly expressed and experimented by no less a world renowned educational thinker and innovator than Rabindranath Tagore? When would we provide our learners and teachers with environ-enriched altars of education where learning and teaching are never jeopardized by the 'brick and mortar arrangements' in order to kill the very impulse of freedom and joy?

Leaving aside the fact that education everywhere is bogged down to a lifeless, dull, drab and mechanical process, thanks a lot to computer-savvy education, the greatest casualty is the unique world of every learner's creative and critical thinking. Our learners in schools today hardly find any favourable avenue or opportunity of exercising individual creative and critical talent. Nor do our teachers entrusted with the sacred and arduous task of teaching do justice to minimum desirable individualized instruction primarily because they are more interested in completing the syllabus than in exploring and cultivating newer strategies of quality education for creative and innovative advancement of learning. That justice is appallingly denied to pupil-curiosity and critical thinking is exposed in the crowded atmosphere of heterogeneous classroom teaching where generalized patterns and procedures of imparting instructions terribly tell upon freedom of exercise and, thereafter, evaluation of individuality. Under the circumstances, the psychological principle of individualizing instructions and at the same time appropriate socialization of learners becomes a catch phrase with no bearing on or evidence to efflorescence of individuality. Meanwhile, overhauling any system of education by overlooking all these deficiencies as evident from recent trends in secondary education has simply aggravated maladies in organization, administration and supervision.

As regards the complex scenario of national and evolutionary vision of education for natural and spontaneous efflorescence of learning, the ills of education have so much diluted and damaged the fundamental aims and objectives that any attempt at reshuffling whatsoever in the arena of teaching-learning has more or less been subject to debate and undesirable resentment. Waging a war as it were against private tuitions by teachers and engaging them to remain in the school campus beyond work- schedule have severely affected smooth running of academic and allied programmes of activities. Who denies that minimum working facilities are not available for teachers in many schools where they can uninterruptedly deal with correction of pupils' written exercises, counselling and guidance notwithstanding? Apposite utilization of off periods are ironically replaced by careless and passive hibernation in slumber and aggravating wastage of intellectual promise and perfection in the solemn assignment of meaningful, purposeful, resourceful and, above all, worthwhile and humane teaching for an ideal and thrilling school climate.

Arresting teacher efficiency and teacher involvement without prior organisation of holding a favourable and effective dialogue between the teaching community and the administrative bureaucrats is like scaffolding sane thoughts and challenging priorities in education for ascent and excellence. In fact, the recent stricture on teachers with regard to private tuitions is, as some educationists of eminence would observe, by and large a whimsical and perhaps redundant and slovenly approach very likely to putting the cart before the horse in the name of academic revolution. Needless to mention, such an approach buoyantly breeds the dangerous seeds of violence and disintegration in the school climate. As an inevitable consequence, the hapless learners are the worst sufferers for practically no fault of their own. Moreover, the reasons for absence of apposite teaching -learning climate remain far from being considered with a little bit of sympathy and earnestness, patience and seriousness.

Admittedly, apathy and ignorance in the arena of secondary education are the most vulnerable areas jeopardising all avenues of progress in teaching-learning climate. When education aims at advancement of learning for the limited few and not for all, revamping the school climate becomes almost illusory and absolutely meaningless. It smacks at being partial, parochial, fragmentary, biased and value-shy. A casual look at the present syllabus of secondary education will present everyone with some glaring loopholes. It betrays the minimum essentials of language learning for satisfactorily negotiating working knowledge and for higher learning. Secondly, absence of coordination and synchronisation of different syllabi at different stages of learning has allowed ample learning gaps detrimental to a balanced and scientific advancement of learning. Thirdly, many teachers are at crossroads with the ambiguous and, more often than not, redundant matters of teaching different topics. Fourthly, the courses of studies are in some subjects baseless and far below the standard. Consequently, there is hardly any scope for exploring newer avenues of teaching-learning.

Paradoxically, in the name of revamping secondary education, secondary matters such as banning of private tuitions by teachers are given primary importance while improvements of textbooks, libraries, laboratories, and, above all, classrooms well-equipped with necessary and desirable teaching aids are yet to be given due importance and weightage. The results are obvious. Pupils with either starved or half-baked learning are terribly becoming misfits not only in education but also in day-to-day affairs of life. This is not all. They also are prone to become an easy prey to anti-socials with whose stubborn and contagious grooming they are forced to learn the dangerous lessons of vandalism, hooliganism, terrorism and numerous other activities that tarnish the very image of man as a responsible social being. Indiscipline and ukase have become a regular affair in educational institutions under their forceful and massive control in such a way as to launch strikes, *bandhs, gheraos, dharnas* and several other disruptive strategies sufficient for compelling education to take an undisturbed backseat.

Learning what and how to teach ought to be given a look afresh and anew. Keeping in view the primary ends-in-view of reviving the school climate in the context of the present-day needs and priorities, there ought to be a symphony between different disciplines and teaching competence. As the Report to UNESCO of the International Commission on Education for the Twenty-first Century rightly observes:

> The world is evolving so rapidly today that teachers, like most other professional groups, now must face the fact that their initial training will not see them through the rest of their lives: they need to update and improve their own knowledge and techniques throughout their lifetime. A careful balance has to be struck between competence in the subject taught and competence in teaching. In some countries, the system is criticised for neglecting method; in others,

> overemphasis on method, it is felt, produces teachers who know too little about their subject. Both are needed; neither should be sacrificed to the other in initial or in-service training. Teacher training has additionally to inculcate a view of teaching that transcends the utilitarian and encourages questioning, interaction and consideration of several alternative hypotheses.
>
> — *Learning: The Treasure Within*, UNESCO Publishing, 1996, p. 149

Along with the cultivation and maintenance of a careful and cautious balance between subject and teaching in accelerating teacher competency, good-quality training of teachers for effective school administration, supervision and guidance is essential. Let the school principals in particular be equipped with the latest trends and techniques of effective school management. Let a new aura of excellence in the school climate be fine tuned with sincere devotion and dedication to sensitive obligations like endearingly handling students, teachers and others associated with education. Linking parents and guardians with educational plans and programmes of activities with a view to consolidate better school climate is not only desirable but also obligatory. As the Commission referred to earlier significantly suggests:

> A good school head who is capable of establishing effective teamwork, and is seen as being competent and open-minded often achieves major

> improvements in the quality of his or her school. Care should therefore be taken to ensure that headships go to qualified professionals who have had special training, in management in particular. This training should result in school principals being given increased responsibilities and adequate remuneration for the discharge of their sensitive obligations. In the context of education throughout life, where everyone is in turn teacher and learner, people from outside the profession who are recruited for fixed periods or specific tasks can bring into schools certain skills that are needed and not available among the teaching staff—teaching in minority languages, teaching refugees, or linking education more closely with the world of work, for example. Involving parents in teaching activities in collaboration with trained teachers has in some circumstances proved to be a useful factor in improving school attendance, the quality of teaching and social cohesion.
>
> — *Ibid*, p. 151

The aesthetics of the school climate necessitates practice in all purity and poignance right now. The cathedral of awareness to truth, beauty and goodness beckons us. An all-embracing catholicity of vision in all affairs of education is the need of the hour. *Ah noh bhadra kratava yantu visvata*—let noble thoughts come to us from every side. The rest is fullness of man through fullness in education.

It is high time to address some of the crucial issues with regard to planning and management of school education bearing in mind that unless transparency in every component is assured, no significant progress in education is possible. In this connection, the following guidelines deserve sincere consideration:

(a) Evolving a long-term planning and management perspective of education and its integration with the country's developmental and manpower needs.

(b) Decentralisation and the creation of a spirit of autonomy for educational institutions.

(c) Giving pre-eminence to pupil's involvement, including association of non-governmental agencies and voluntary effort.

(d) Inducting more women in the planning and management of education.

(e) Establishing the principle of accountability in relation to given objectives and norms.

—*National Policy on Education-1986* (With Modifications Undertaken in 1992), Ministry of Human Resource Development, Department of Education, New Delhi, 1992, Publication No.

1723, p. 45.

Planning for educational development programmes should also encompass the interests of rural and remote areas from where many students do not receive appropriate impetus for advancement of learning. Moreover, the resources, infrastructure opportunities and facilities are to be retuned for the benefit of really interested and deserving students. The problems of stop-outs also await newer programming and processing of planned activities that should be truly relevant and meaningful, dynamic and purposeful. The aims and objectives for planning should be presupposed in terms of equity, social justice, free from gender bias, pluralistic and sensitised from individualistic and group ends-in-view of performance and progress.

The function of the common school system also necessitates a rethinking in right earnest from the standpoint of planning and management. Acceleration of disparities in connection with rural and urban schools, private and government schools etc. should be arrested and eliminated. Instead, mutuality in understanding and appreciation by means of folding them under the earnest umbrella of sympathy and co-operation of the common school concept of the School Complex be given a warm welcome of cordial acceptance.

Admittedly, any dynamic planning should be forewarned with the following pregnant observations:

> The rural areas in general, and the tribal areas in particular, have suffered in terms of resources, personnel and infrastructure facilities. This phenomenon of regional disparities in

educational development has acquired a major political dimension in the current Indian scene. It is reflected in the regional and sub-regional movements. Therefore, the need of the hour is planning for, and implementation of, educational developmental programmes in terms of disaggregated targets and, area, community and gender specific activities. This would mean concrete programmes being established on ground for the disadvantaged groups—SCs and Tribes, women, the educationally minorities and the handicapped with appropriate budgeting for the same. No doubt, there have been special component plans for the SCs and sub-plans for the Tribes. But these plans have largely remained exercises on paper, not concretely provided for the budget documents. The consequence has been that these plans have not had any impact on the educational standards of the SCs and STs in terms of enrolment, retention and reduction in drop out rates. Excepting for the implementation of a small Scheme, "The Integrated Education for the Disabled", the handicapped do not significantly feature in the educational programmes of the Centre or the States. The Programmes for the educationally backward minorities have not been significant, having been construed as

> the almost exclusive domain of the States.
>
> In order to promote participation of the girls and women at all levels, there is need for an integrated approach in designing and implementing the Schemes that would address all the factors that inhibit their education. Mere implementation of disaggregated schemes such as Opening of Non-Formal Education Centres for Women etc. by themselves are not adequate. In this context special mention may be made of inter-action of Early Childhood Care and Education (ECCE) with primary education. Education of women is not to be construed of a question of mere access but of empowering them through education of all through equality of sexes.
>
> —*Towards an Enlightened and Humane Society,* Report of the Committee for Review of National Policy on Education (NPE), 1986, Final Report, p. 15.

As regards planning in education for development of values, we will have to go many more miles in achieving our objectives of education for fullness. As a matter of fact, problems like value dilemmas and value clarifications more often than not present us with delicate and critical constraints of education in an ideal setting of well managed activities. In this regard, learning values by living demands planned activities in every school, where the source points. viz., the school as an institution, community and agent of community developments as suggested by Seshadri and Khader:

- *School as an Institution (School Rules, Regulations, Customs, Traditions, Rituals, Hidden Curriculum, etc.)*
- Student Self-government—Election, oath-taking, school parliament or assem-bly, etc.
- School assembly, student meetings
- Celebration of festivals, national days, other important days and occasions
- School institutions and mechanisms to carry out its various functions, especially discipline
- School Day
- Convocation day
- School and class organisation for instruction and other activities—seating arrangements in class, etc.

School as a Community

- Cleaning the school rooms, school premises, hostels
- Levelling the playground
- Preparing and maintaining a school garden
- Decorating the classroom and the school
- Polishing the furniture

- Whitewashing the walls
- Painting the doors and windows
- Help in the preparation of school meals
- Help in serving and other hostel work
- School excursions
- School camps and workshops on various themes: literary, national integration, population education, environment, etc.
- Help school children in their studies, etc.

School as an Agent of Community Development

- Organising campaigns on sanitation, cleanliness, health and nutrition, alcoholism, literacy, women and children, population, environment, care of animals (surveys, *padyatras*, demonstrations, street plays, etc.)
- Participation in community development activities, construction works (roads, wells, tanks, buildings), harvesting, social forestry
- Service to the needy, helping the aged and sick, helping in adult education
- Carrying out relief activities during natural disasters, accidents, riots, —first aid, blood donation

- Enriching life in the community—participation and organisation of recreational activities, cultural programmes, etc.

–C. Seshadri and M. A. Khader: "Practical Methods and Approaches—Illustrative Activities", *Education in Values: A Source Book*, National Council of Educatio-nal Research and Training, New Delhi, 1992, p. 202.

Planning and management of school for learning in and through Nature can hardly be overestimated. In fact, the importance of the open plan for a school for natural and spontaneous development in an atmosphere of freedom and creativity is the only means of justifying education living, meaningful and full of the promise of success in growth and development of personality.

As a pioneer in cultivation of education for fulness, the contributions of Rabindranath Tagore are immense. His thoughts and experiments on planning the school as an abode of the study of the mind of man in its realisation of whatever stands as a pointer to excellence are still relevant. As he characteristically remarks:

> The primary object of an institution should not be merely to educate one's limbs and mind to be in efficient readiness for all emergencies, but to be in perfect tune in the symphony of

response between life and world, to find the balance of their harmony which is wisdom. The first important lesson for children in such a place would be that of improvisation, the constant imposition of the ready-made having been banished from here. It is to give occasions to explore one's capacity through surprises of achievement. I must make it plain that this means a lesson not in simple life, but in creative life. For life may grow complex, and yet if there is a living personality in its centre, it will still have the unity of creation; it will carry its own weight in perfect grace, and will not be a mere addition to the number of facts that only goes to swell a crowd.

I wish I could say that I had fully realised my dream in my school. I have only made the first introduction towards it and have given an opportunity to the children to find their freedom in Nature by being able to love it. For love is freedom; it gives us that fullness of existence which saves us from paying with our soul for objects that are immensely cheap. Love lights up this world with its meaning and makes life feel that it has that "enough" everywhere which truly is its "feast". I know men who preach the cult of simple life by glorifying the spiritual merit of poverty. I refuse to imagine any special value in poverty when it is a mere negation. Only when the mind has the sensitiveness to be able to respond to the deeper call of reality is it naturally weaned away from the lure of the fictitious value of things. It is callousness which robs us of our simple power to enjoy, and dooms us to the indignity of a snobbish pride in furniture and the foolish burden of expensive things. But the callousness of asceticism pitted against the callousness of luxury is merely fighting one evil with the help of another, inviting the pitiless demon of the desert in the place of the indiscriminate demon of the jungle.

I tried my best to develop in the children of my school the freshness of their feeling for Nature, a sensitiveness of soul in their relationship with their human surroundings, with the help of literature, festive ceremonials and also the religious teaching which enjoins us to come to the nearer presence of the world through the soul, thus to gain it more than can be measured—like gaining an instrument in truth by bringing out its music.

—Rabindranath Tagore: "The Teacher", *The Religion of Man,* George Allen & Unwin Ltd, London, 1953, pp. 178-180.

When would we tune the school climate to bring out its music?

10

Value Education for Socio-Aesthetic Excellence: The Indian Context

Education is a way of life. Value education is a specific and significant way of how to lead one's life as one ought to lead in order to be justified to others as well as to oneself. It is a pointer to one's development in diverse dimensions—physical, mental, emotional, social, aesthetic, cultural and so on. It also indicates how to direct and diversify the essence of life so that education really becomes a natural and spontaneous vehicle of efflorescence of one's desirable and worthwhile personality.

Education is also concerned with excellence. Unlike any other channel of excellence, values cultivated in and through education direct one to ascent and excellence. Unless ascent and excellence become the end-in-view of education, it becomes a mere tool for toying with the drab realities of life that kill the finer sensibilities of every item of knowledge and experience. Moreover, knowledge to be purified and poised in depth of vision and promise and perfume of fullness always awaits the preparation and practice of the right mind of the right kind at the right moment of self-illumination that indicates the success of education as a characteristic medium of excellence.

That values in life today have been severely affected by reasons due to our aggravating aspirations and sky kissing life style is undeniable. The socio-aesthetic excellence that we want to receive through education for values has been at continual crossroads with our increasing love for newer things and commodities without which we equate education with meaninglessness and bereft of any worth. In this connection, one recalls Fromm's priceless evaluation of man:

> Man today is fascinated by the possibility of buying more, better, and especially, new things. He is consumption-hungry. The act of buying and consuming has become a compulsive, irrational aim, because it is in an end in itself, with little relation to the use of, or pleasure in the things bought or consumed. To buy the latest gadget, the latest model of anything that is on the market, is the dream of everybody, in comparison to which the real pleasure in use is quite secondary. Modern man, if he dared to be articulate about his concept of heaven, would describe a vision which would look like the biggest department store in the world, showing new things and gadgets, and himself having plenty of money with which to buy them. He

> would wander around open-mouthed in the heaven of gadgets and commodities, provided only that there were ever more and newer things to but, and perhaps his neighbors were just a little less privileged than he.
>
> —Erich Fromm: *The Sane Society,* Holt, Rinehart Winston, 1955, p. 135.

Meanwhile devaluation of values throughout the world has posed a serious threat to survival of man as a socio-aesthetic being. The four significant areas of human attachments viz., society, mass disaster through war, economic imbalance and, above all, eugenics—thanks to the so-called modern civilisation blessed with science and technology of the latest kinds—are really posing threats to all finer values and nobler sentiments of life. As Bell categorically elucidates:

> *War prevention.* While the odds against another war within the next generation are considered to be 80 percent (within 25 years), a 20 percent chance is intolerable. The main appears to be in mutually undesired escalation and downright inadvertence; hence a major effort to seek improved ways of forestalling such disaster becomes necessary.
>
> *Equitable distribution of resources.* While there is a consensus that eventually there will be an abundance of resources in energy, food, and raw materials, there is no foregone conclusion that such resources will be

available in time for the increasing world population, or that effective means of an equitable world distribution will have been found and agreed upon. To solve such problems would clearly be a great contribution toward the prevention of big or small wars.

Social reorganisation. The anticipated growth in the amount of automation is likely to reshape the industrialized nations. While improved and highly automated methods of education will make the acquisition of technical skills available to a larger fraction of the population, only the very ablest people are likely to be needed to manage the new, automated economy. Since robots are apt to take over many of the services, especially the more menial ones, large segments of the population may find themselves without suitable employment within an economy of potential abundance. Farsighted and profoundly revolutionary measures may have to be taken to cope with this situation.

Eugenics. Finally, a problem, though not yet upon us, which will require much forethought and wisdom. There is the possibility—within a generation or two—of selectively extending an individual's life span through biochemical methods and of selective eugenic control through molecular genetic engineering.

— Daniel Bell: *"The Study of the Future"*,

The Public Interest, Vol. I, No. 1, Fall 1965, p. 130.

Value education as it is understood, accepted and practised in India from time immemorial has the most incomparable and unparalleled distinction of crystallizing the way and vision of life in terms of Indian socio-aesthetics. Unfortunately, due to an undesirable system of education which has its long and painful history in India, education for values in general and socio-aesthetic values in particular suffered a lot:

- First, education for self-reliance and self-identity has not been allowed to thrive under the pressure of foreign values and foreign culture.
- Second, the finer elements of value education for reducing oneself to a cipher for the cause of others as one of the most significant points of departure on value education for socio-aesthetic excellence has been severely jeopardised.
- Third, the selfless culture of the aesthetics of social oneness even by exercising the education of individual growth and development and vice versa has practically been allowed to enjoy passivity and abject carelessness.
- Fourth, value-transfers today fight shy of the minimum essence of cultivation of socio-aesthetic crystallization of consciousness.

Where is the assured promise and perfume of perfection so much so that a certain sense of catholicity of refinement and excellence becomes the characteristic essence of education that evolves in freedom, spontaneity and creativity, coordination, culture and continuity?

Why do we emphasize specially on values in education as these have been nurtured in India from time to time? Why should our children be provided with the nursling of education that cares for idealising and practising those socio-aesthetic values that form the basics of excellence and ascent of man? How can we revive and initiate these essential socio-aesthetic values in course of our every pattern of educational endeavour at any time and every time anywhere and everywhere? Undeniably, these are some of the vital issues of the present-day education in India where education is terribly failing to arrest and ward off erosion of essential socio-aesthetic values in particular. As a matter of fact, today's education looks askance at cultivation of values for social and aesthetic awareness under the ukase of life, wisdom and knowledge so marvellously spelt out in volleys of queries by T S Eliot:

Where is the life we have lost in living?
Where is the wisdom we have lost in knowledge?
Where is the knowledge we have lost in information?

—"Choruses From the Rock"

The essential components of values in education for efflorescence of socio-aesthetic excellence as practised and enriched from time to time in India necessitate a re-thinking and re-cultivation in right earnest right now. What is really very thrilling, interesting and rejuvenating in the very concept of education for acceleration of aesthetics in terms of individual and social development is that in the Indian system of education there are some unique and apposite theories, which, if practised with all devotion and sincerity of purpose, would contribute a lot to education for fullness. The quest for socio-aesthetic values in and through education as enkindled from the Indian text is based on education that liberates one from all odds and constraints of achieving fullness—*Sa vidya ya vimuktaye.* Again, education for cultivation as socio-aesthetic values cannot be exercised unless it is well strengthened by total involvement and devotion, sincerity and unending sticktoitiveness to questionings and service—*Pranipatena pariprasnena sevaya.*

The backdrop of value education for socio-aesthetic advancement and excellence from the Indian context as above also welcomes some other characteristic features which may be introduced in the day-to-day educational activities in a two-fold way either by an individual learner or by a group of learners as follows:

- **The External Way**

This may include, in school education in particular, the following activities for cultivation of aesthetic sensibilities:

(a) Decorating the classrooms with paintings, pictures of eminent personalities, drawings of *alpanas,* sketches and the like.

(b) Appropriate use of flowers and foliages, earthen wares, lamps etc.

(c) Welcoming and honouring the revered guests with sandal pastes, flower garlands, fragrance of incense, blowing of conch-shells, and *Uttariyas* and other types of

Angabastras or dress materials symbolic of aesthetic awareness.

(d) Chanting of Vedic hymns, reading out relevant extracts from illustrious personalities.

(e) Singing choric songs to unfold the conjoint and communicated experience of socio-aesthetic values.

The Internal Way

As regards this way, the following are some of the essential socio-aesthetic values that necessitate regular and sincere practice in every form and strategy of educational endeavour:

(a) Service to the poor and the disadvantaged, the downtrodden and the neglected, the dishonoured and the belittled.

(b) Practice of humility and reverence, modesty and warm embrace to one and all irrespective of caste, creed, community, race, religion, complexion, nationality etc. whatsoever.

(c) Appreciating truth, beauty and goodness as invaluable components of socio-aesthetic serenity of poignance.

(d) Exercising joy, freedom and creativity in terms of socio-aesthetic fulfilment of the inner essence and excellence of humans.

(e) Devoting steadfastly to the finer socio-aesthetic nuances of tolerance, magnanimity and aus-terity, perseverance, righteousness and simplicity.

One can go on some other values and the components/sub-components thereof contributing directly or indirectly to advancement of socio-aesthetic sensibilities, but what is primarily needed in the pursuit of education specially for the young learners in schools is to see how far these call forth a spontaneous and three approach in nursling of humane values both subjectively and objectively. In fact, all endeavour education for cultivation and enrichment of socio-aesthetic values should better be *caught* instead of being *taught* as it is more or less done in course of teaching of values of any kind of any stage whatsoever or howsoever.

Admittedly, the teaching of values in general and socio-aesthetic values in particular is a very challenging and difficult task. The strategies ought to be clearly, precisely and correctly spelt out. The clientele learners' attitude, curiosity, interest, ability to interpret and appreciate diverse and different socio-aesthetic values in terms of comparison and contrast, response and response, elasticity and dissemination are also to be entertained as significant sources-points of depth of inward vision.

The role of the teacher in the teaching of socio-aesthetic values is legion. She/He ought herself/himself pursue and devote to the study of socio-aesthetics creatively and critically. She/He ought to sincerely carry out the duties and responsibilities of a teacher to enkindle the learning lamps of her/his learners to the best of her/his abilities and teaching competence. She/He ought not to loseself-confidence restraint in tone and temper as all these destroy the cocoon as it were of the socio-aesthetic values of excellence inherent in every learner.

Truly, there is no short cut to teaching of socio-aesthetic values. At the same time, the strategies adopted by the teacher do not necessarily guarantee success in teaching. Sometimes it may so happen that these strategies demand tailoring in the apposite fashion best suited to the needs and possibilities of effulgence of socio-aesthetic consciousness of value-study and value-evaluation in terms of value-appreciation by means of individual creative and aesthetic thinking on idealisation, interpretation, synchronisation, elimination, reinforcement and feedback of values associated with man and society.

A checklist of dos and don'ts on teaching of values for socio-aesthetic excellence may include the following:

(i) Is the content-matter foolproof, relevant, interesting, appealing and vibrant to learners?

(ii) Does the teacher herself/himself find the joy of associating herself/himself with her/his pupils in exploring and experimenting upon newer avenues of value education for social development and aesthetic appreciation?

(iii) Is the teaching-learning atmosphere congenial to exercise value education?

(iv) What response do teachers and students receive apart from their own institutions?

(v) What are the vulnerable areas of introducing value education and what are the immediate and long-term strategies for smooth functioning of teaching for value orientation?

(vi) What are the prospects of networking training and orientation of teachers and teacher educators for the specific purpose of teaching social sensibilities and aesthetics of values in education?

(vii) What are the assessment and accreditation programmes associated with teaching and learning of socio-aesthetic values?

Indeed, the logistics of education for value learning, value teaching, value identification, value analysis, value appreciation, value synchronisation, value assessment and accreditation always await redefining, re-crystallising and re-disseminating in the saner thought thoughts and nobler visions of advancement of culture and civilisation.

Excellence in the arena of value culture is an adventure strenuous but thrilling, difficult but dividend paying. What is needed is earnestness and seriousness of purpose to be rightly directed towards creating a solemn platform of *vidyasamavaya* or cooperation of learning, *vidyavinimaya* or exchange of learning, *vidyayachai* or justification of learning, *vidyamulyayana* or evaluation of learning and *vidyavikirana* or dissemination of learning.

From the socio-aesthetic points of view, education for values must admit the fact that in our very nature and habit, in attitude and dwarfing of values lie our destruction and doom. Let the blessings of socio-aesthetic values imparted through education allow every one of us to hold our heads high, minds unbiased, ambitions ardent, promises pure and perfect, and goals to reach the pinnacle of glories. Let us be reborn with that undaunted spirit of socio-aesthetics which knows no defeat or littleness and which, on the other hand, teaches us how to serve every one of the global society to the best of our abilities: *Sarve sukhinoh bhavantu sarve santu niramayah*—Let every one of us be happy, let every one be sans any malady.

Betwixt the cultural man and the aesthetic man values make a new beginning and a new meaning where the differences are merged in terms of ascent and excellence. In fact, human contemplation and action always look forward to beginning a new platform of humanity where education directs one to make an unending quest for values. Only then free development of human consciousness by means of a happy unison between intelligent aspirations and apposite reasoning prizes man with ascent and excellence. As Sri Aurobindo remarkably elucidates:

> Not to live principally in the activities of the sense-mind, but in the activities of knowledge and reason and a wide intellectual curiosity, the activities of the enlightened will which make for character and high ethical ideals and a large human action, not to be governed by our lower or our average mentality but by truth and beauty and by the self-ruling will is the ideal of a true culture and the beginning of an accomplished humanity. But still on

> this higher plane we are apt to be pursued by old exclusiveness and misunderstandings—the frequent quarrel between culture and conduct, between Hebraism and Hellenism. The source of the conflict arises from the triangular disposition of the higher or more subtle mentality: a side of will, conduct, character which creates the ethical man, and another side of sensibility to the beautiful which creates the aesthetic man, looking askance at each other with mutual distrust or even reprobation. Society is only an enlargement of the individual and the contrast and opposition reproduces itself in social and national types.... Neither the ethical being nor the aesthetic being is the whole man, nor can either be his sovereign principle. They must be taken up and enlightened by a higher principle capable of understanding both equally, their purposes and potentialities. That higher principle seems to be provided for us by the human faculty of reason and intelligent will.
>
> • Sri Aurobindo: *The Human Cycle,* Sri Aurobindo Pathamandir, Calcutta, 1972, pp. 30-32.

Values for socio-aesthetic excellence always necessitate an emancipation of the self. Unless there is a quest for the Infinite within oneself, the All Serene remains far away from every 'I'. Hence, the highest end-in-view of socio-aesthetic excellence ought to seek and seek the endless path of poignance and perfection. As Tagore christens us:

> It is the very characteristic of life that it is not complete within itself; it must come out. Its truth is in the commerce of the inside and the outside. In order to live, the body must maintain its various relations with the outside light and air—not only to gain life-force, but also to manifest it. Consider how fully employed the body is with its own inside activities; its heart-beat must not stop for a second, its stomach, its brain, must be ceaselessly working. Yet this is not enough; the body outwardly restless all the while. Its life leads it to an endless dance of work and play outside; it cannot be satisfied with the circulations of its internal economy, and only finds the fulfilment of joy in its outward excursions.
>
> —Rabindranath Tagore: "Realisation in Action", *Sadhana*, Macmillan India Limited, New Delhi, 1988, p. 105.

Meanwhile, let every one of us, prior to making any endeavour at education for socio-aesthetic excellence and ascent of values, join the prayer for light:

> Light, oh where is the light? Kindle it with the burning fire of desire!
>
> There is the lamp but never the flicker of a flame—is such thy fate, my heart? Ah, death were better by far for thee!

> Misery knocks at thy door, and her message is that thy lord is wakeful, and he calls thee to the love-tryst through the darkness of night.
>
> The sky is overcast with clouds and the rain is ceaseless. I know not what this is that stirs in me –I know not its meaning.
>
> A moment's flash of lightning drags down a deeper gloom on my sight, and my heart gropes for the path to where the music of the night calls me.
>
> Light, oh where is the light! Kindle it with the burning fire of desire! It thunders and the wind rushes screaming through the void. The night is black as a black stone. Let not the hours pass by in the dark. Kindle the lamp of love with thy life.
>
> —Rabindranath Tagore: *Gitanjali,* Macmillan India Limited, New Delhi, Macmillan Pocket Tagore Edition, 1983, No. XXVII, pp. 15-16.

When would we be worthy of justifying Indian values in education in the light of life and love?

Index